44 (R.M.) COMMANDO

Achnacarry to the Arakan: A Diary of the
Commando at War, August 1943 to March
1947

Tony Mackenzie
With a Foreword by Major General J.I.H.Owen OBE

Tom Donovan
Brighton

First published in 1996 by

Tom Donovan Publishing Ltd.
2 Newport Street
Brighton
East Sussex BN2 3HL

ISBN: 1-871085-33-0

Desk-top typeset by Tom Donovan Publishing Ltd.

Printed by The Bath Press, Bath

Contents

Seven maps and 23 illustrations will be found in the text

Author's Introduction and Acknowledgments

I was three years of age when my eldest brother returned home on leave after completing the Commando Course with 44 at Achnacarry in 1943. Six weeks later the family bade him a fond farewell and it was almost another three years before he returned from the Far East. Over the intervening years I have relished listening to comical reminiscences of the Achnacarry experience, the sea trips and train journeys, the trials and tribulations of the Burma campaign and stories of the runs ashore (mostly unprintable) in India, Ceylon and Hong Kong.

Whilst researching another subject at the Public Record Office at Kew I stumbled upon the war diaries of 44. I browsed through the pages and, recognising names and places mentioned in numerous conversations over the years, decided to jot down a few facts and figures with a view of compiling a brief resume of the unit's travels during WW2. However, the more I delved into the war diaries, the more absorbed I became in 44's history, and like Topsy my notes grew and grew and grew... and this book was born.

I am indebted to several people whose invaluable assistance is much appreciated:

My brother Laurie and our 'oppo' for over 50 years Arthur Pengelly. They educated me in what it means to be a Royal Marine, their pride in being part of 44 is as apparent now as it was all those years ago. These two 'Royals' are a testament to the Commando buddy system, they still meet on a weekly basis to put the world to rights over a few pints of beer.

Mr Steve Murrell for perusing the first few chapters and gently reminding me as to precisely where capital letters, commas and full stops should be inserted.

Three ex-officers of 44:

Capts Peter Parish and Edward Sturges who provided excellent and entertaining lunches, passed on a wealth of detailed information and gave me their unqualified support, so important to a novice author. Capt Headley Phillips kindly made available many of the photographs used in this book.

The family of Royal Marines also provided a proof-reader, Mr Don Denby (Secretary of the London Branch, Royal Marines Association) and Mr Alan Waite (ex-44) who enhanced the quality of the photographs.

By the time this story had reached the 60,000 word mark my brother suggested that "perhaps John Owen would be interested." I am bound to say that without the help, guidance, and encouragement given to me by Major General Owen I doubt whether this book would have been produced. Not only was he always on hand to answer my many questions, he put names to faces, provided the necessary introductions to interested parties and painstakingly scrutinised the manuscript, line by line, to check for accuracy, amend where necessary and advise on the correct military terms and abbreviations used in the text.

FOREWORD
by
Maj Gen J.I.H.OWEN OBE

The story of 44(RM)Cdo or "Four Four" as we called ourselves is chronicled in the pages that follow. It is the story of a Commando which was tempered at Achnacarry, welded together at Kedgaon and Alethangyaw, and proved in the fire at Kangaw where its brave defence of 'Pinner' lies in the shadow of the brave deeds on Hill 170.

It is difficult to describe adequately the heat and humidity, the fevers, prickly heat and jungle sores, the moments of loneliness, sadness and humour, the austerity and arduous training and last, but not least, the challenge of India, Ceylon and Burma. These and other experiences, including worries about our families at home, could have been a source of friction and trouble, but the discipline, sense of purpose and the infectious humour of the self-reliant Commando marine held us together. In any case, we all had a job to do. We also had the comradeship and rivalry between the battle-hardened Five, our Army Commando friends, and the strong fit, but less experienced, Four Four to keep us on our toes. All these reflections can be found directly or between the lines of this excellent diary.

Many of the actors on the Four Four stage are sadly no longer with us, but I hope that those who remain will, by reading this Diary, recall some forgotten moments of their young lives. Above all they can share these moments with their families who otherwise may never know what they endured in the service of Four Four and of our country.

Tony Mackenzie has researched meticulously and untiringly on his self-imposed mission to write the story of Four Four. He has written a wonderfully memorable and easy reading account. I hope that those who read it will be as grateful to him as I am for this Diary.

September 1995

1
Formation and Training

Shortly after the start of the Second World War a Royal Marine Division (101, 102 and 103 RM Brigades) was formed and subsequently used in a 'home defence' role. The RM Division was one of the very few formations which, after Dunkirk, was capable of providing a defence should the German Army have mounted its expected attack. It was not until the threat of invasion had passed in 1941 that the marines could be used for other purposes. The division, although well-trained, hardy and rearing to go, lacked supporting weapons and front line reinforcements. It had been earmarked for several operations but, mainly because of these shortcomings, had been denied the opportunity when the time came.

Meanwhile, Army Commandos had been raised and integrated into the Army structure. Early operations against targets on enemy held coastlines and islands demonstrated the need for more such units. At the time conventional army units could ill-afford to lose volunteers wishing to transfer to the Commandos. Lord Louis Mountbatten had been appointed Chief of Combined Operations in March 1942 and as a naval officer was well aware of the Royal Marines potential; he saw that the RM Division was a ready source of manpower that could be used to provide the additional Commandos needed. From the 7000 officers, NCOs and marines of the Division and 3000 from other sources, 40% were allocated to Commando units.

As a result of the subsequent reorganisation of the RM Division, 44(RM) Commando was formed from the 3rd Battalion on 1st August 1943. Together with the other designated battalions of the RM Division they would pass through the Commando Depot at Achnacarry to be trained to perform the Commando Role. References at the time inferred that the Royal Marines tradition of landing from the sea had been appropriated by the Army Commandos. There was some initial opposition from within the Corps to the new assignment, especially as the marines were to operate in conjunction with their army counterparts. As part of 101 Brigade RM, the 3rd Battalion had been training in Wales and Scotland (including time spent at the Combined Operations Training Centre at Inveraray). The average bootneck[1] was unconcerned with the politics involved.

Most had already volunteered to join the Corps in the first instance and felt that they were well qualified to become Commando soldiers.

Corps history told him that it was the Royal Marines of the 4th Battalion who on St Georges Day 1918 had stormed the mole at Zeebrugge. Such widespread heroism was witnessed on that day that every man in the Battalion was ballotted to be awarded one of the two Victoria Crosses that were bestowed on the marines that took part in the action.

This action was a commando raid personified.

On the day that 3RM became 44 (RM) Commando its personnel marched past the new unit flag before attending a church service held in the NAAFI. A message of 'Best wishes' was received from Brig A.N.Williams RM, commander, 101 Brigade RM and on 6th August 1943 Lt Col F.C.Horton RM assumed command of 44.

Ashurst
1st August–6th September 1943

44 (RM) Commando officers 1st August 1943

CO	Lt Col F.C. Horton
2IC	Major J.L.Macafee
Adjt	Capt O.St.J.Hamlin MBE
QM	Capt T.C.Coole
IO	Lt A.H.Archer
MO	Capt C.A.McCleary RAMC
Sigs Offr	Lt Arthur Martin

A TROOP	B TROOP
Capt G.P.Sealy	Capt E.M.Sturges
Lt J.I.H.Owen	Lt P.H.Rider
Lt A.E.Barrett	2/Lt S.G.Wintgens

C TROOP	D TROOP
Capt N.J.Winter	Capt K.Martin
Lt A.V.Macan	Lt W.J.Standing
Lt A.R.White	2/Lt P.T.Musters

---

1   Slang word meaning Royal Marine. Sailors of the Nelson era originally gave the name to marines, the neck of their red tunics being lined with leather (hence US marines being known as 'Leathernecks').

X TROOP	S TROOP
Capt K.P.Parish	Capt R.G.Steele
Lt C.N.Carryer	Lt K.A.Abbs
Lt S.Henshall	

At Ashurst the training routine was intensified, having the three main aims that:

1. all individuals were capable of carrying out their own task and the tasks of any other man in the unit;

2. every man in the unit was to be made disciplinarily self-reliant;

3. the unit be prepared to undertake arduous training at the Commando Depot, Achnacarry.

It was recognised that the forthcoming specialist training would test each man's fitness and endurance to the utmost. The first Training Directive contained disciplines and tests that each man would have to pass. Of the eleven tests of fitness laid down, at least eight had to be successfully completed by every officer and marine. All ranks were expected to be able to complete a 15 mile march in three hours wearing fighting order and carrying ammunition for all weapons.

The standard of marksmanship would be raised by extensive use of the ranges. It was noted at the time that trained Commando units contained few second class shots, whereas 44 had little else. The drive to classify all ranks as first-class shots took on an air of utmost urgency. With the pressure on, the ride across the ranges in three-ton trucks travelling at breakneck speed made many marines wonder if they would still be alive when the trucks stopped at the rifle butts!

Speed marching by day and night; close-order drill; climbing; weapons and field training; swimming and street fighting were all undertaken with a vengeance. Individual responsibilities, self-reliance, initiative were all qualities being emphasised and encouraged.

The unit's officers undertook the same tasks as the marines, wore the same kit and carried the same weapons. Every officer, NCO and marine was aware that as individuals, all were required to uphold the reputation of the Corps in both discipline and turnout. All troops went swimming in Southampton, the marines speed-marching to the baths.

Orders for the move to Achnacarry were received on the 26th August 1943. The Commanding Officer addressed the Commando outlining the scope of the training to come. To celebrate the glad tidings, ALL ranks commenced a 'Doubling Week' (running everywhere at all times between 0800-1700hrs) which started on the following Monday.

Organisation of Commando units

The proposed establishment of both Army and Royal Marine Commandos was set by the War Office at 24 officers 437 other ranks.

The total of 461 was to include one officer and five other ranks of the RAMC and the reserve of reinforcements was set at 20%.

A commando unit was comprised of seven separate Troops (Tps) Each commando was organised to provide: Five rifle troops, each consisting of three sections.

One heavy weapons troop equipped with Vickers medium machine guns and 3" Mortars (S Tp).

Commando headquarters (HQ Tp).

*   *   *

During the time at Ashurst a general movement of personnel took place. Officers were appointed to the individual troops. Approximately 200 NCOs and marines were discharged to other units throughout the Corps. Five officers, together with ten other ranks were drafted into the unit.

On 3rd September 1943, the advance party (Capt Coole) left Ashurst for Achnacarry, to be followed on 6th September by the main body of the Commando. Reveille was sounded at 0500hrs: 32 officers with 523 other ranks left Lyndhurst Road railway station in two groups for the long day and overnight journey to the highlands of Scotland. All ranks carried haversack rations for 24 hours, personal and troop weapons (except Vickers machine-guns and 3" mortars), small arms ammunition, full kit plus personal equipment. Two items which had to be left behind in accordance with the Notes on Train Discipline were 'dogs and private bicycles!'

The day before the move north, Mne A.R.Owen of X Tp was killed after being hit by a Jeep driven by an American serviceman.

The Commando Depot

Achnacarry House, the surrounding land, the seat of the Clan Cameron and home of its Chief (Cameron of Lochiel), is set in remote countryside in the West Highlands of Scotland. The nearest railway station is eight miles from the castle at Spean Bridge. The nearest large town in the area is Fort William, 14 miles distant.

English soldiers had last set foot over the threshold of Achnacarry in 1745 when the Duke of Cumberland commanded the Army sent to dispel the dreams of Bonnie Prince Charlie. Before leaving Scotland to return south the English troops burned and ravaged the castle.

Shortly after the outbreak of the Second World War in 1939, the then Laird, Sir Donald Cameron, made his home and estate available for use by the military authorities. When Sir Donald vacated his home, he moved to the small village of Clunes, two miles from Achnacarry, from where he could, and did, keep in touch with the activities which took place on his estate.

Initially the castle accommodated the Holding Unit of the 'Special Training Centre.' Up until early 1942 all the existing Commandos, including 40(RM) and 41(RM), had initiated and been responsible for their own training schemes. With the growth of the Commando units, all future specialist training required to be placed on a more formal footing. A comprehensive and unified syllabus would be instituted and courses held at the newly established Commando Depot at Achnacarry. In 1944 this title was changed to the Commando Basic Training Centre.

The officer chosen to organise and run the Commando Depot was Lt Col Charles E.Vaughan, OBE. He assumed command at its inception in February 1942 and remained in the post until 1945. Charles Vaughan, a Londoner, was an exceptional man. He had joined the Coldstream Guards in 1914 and had served in the ranks throughout the First World War. He gained steady promotion from Private to Regimental Sergeant Major. As an RSM he later transferred into The Buffs (Royal East Kent Regiment), from which he retired in 1935. He was recalled to the Colours in 1940 with the rank of captain. Before taking up his appointment as Commandant at Achnacarry he served as a Commando soldier, becoming the 2i/c of No.4 Commando.

The training devised by the Commandant reflected his view that here was an opportunity for adventure and for the commando soldier to show courage, determination, initiative and spirit. His two guiding principles were that:

> 1) Commandos could march seven miles in one hour if the need arose; and

> 2) every instructor, whom he had personally selected, should be a natural leader of men and be capable of completing any task faster and more accurately than the best of the trainees under instruction.

Lt Col Vaughan was one hundred percent Army. His vast military experience, gained during his service as a private soldier, as a Guards RSM and finally as an officer equipped him to deal with any attempt to meddle in the affairs of the Depot.

Many military commands had a finger in the Achnacarry pie: North

Highland District, Scottish Command, Commando Group HQ, Combined Operations HQ, The Royal Marines and the Admiralty. This old soldier was exceptionally adept at playing one organisation off against another, always to the advantage of his command and the personnel who passed through it.

'Charlie' Vaughan's many unofficial titles included: The Rommel of the North, The Laird of Achnacarry, Earl of Spean, Lord Fort William and The Wolf of Badenoch. Sometimes he was quiet spoken, almost a father figure, but when the occasion arose he could become the imposing Guards RSM that he once was. Yet, he was always ready to adopt new training methods suggested by his staff if he saw merit in an idea.

His appointment is perhaps best summed-up by Lord Louis Mountbatten who said: 'The right place has been found and the right man. Achnacarry could hardly be bettered for the site, and Charles Vaughan could certainly not have been bettered as the man.'

The training and military routines were revolutionary in those times. Officers attending the course were welcomed with the news that:

> a) no batman would be available to attend to their needs. The Commandant took the view that if all Commando officers cleaned their own uniform and equipment they would then know, for future reference, how long it would take their men to complete such chores.

> b) for the individual part of the training, officers would form a section, follow the same syllabus as their men, carry equivalent loads and fire the same weapons.

> c) hot water for bathing was non-existent.

> d) junior officers would be sleeping in tents.

> e) the Chief Instructor could, if he so wished, order extra periods of instruction for the officers in the evenings.

> f) the sum of 1/6d (7p) would be added to mess bills, but officers would not be required to dress for dinner unless it was ordered by the Commandant.

For the General Service marine the living conditions had been encountered before. They slept under canvas and messed together as troops in a mess tent, seated at tables of eight.

Although the Depot insisted on an extremely high standard of individual cleanliness, plus more 'spit and polish' than was perhaps expected, emphasis was also laid on instilling personal discipline as well as the more formal regimentation. The absence of formal punishments was noted. Any misdemeanours committed by an individual, which reflected on his own section, were usually dealt with by his colleagues in their own way. This different form of discipline is well illustrated by an example:

One of 44's marines, going hell for leather over the assault course, swung across a mud filled chasm on a rope. 'Royal's' timing and judgement were suspect on that day as he failed to release the rope to land on the safe bank. The man naturally swung back across the gap, finding that he did not have enough impetus to gain safety. The only course of action open to him was to admit defeat, release the rope and drop into the thick, cold mire.

This display of 'Tarzan' gone wrong was watched by an officer instructor. The unfortunate marine's lasting memory of the event is of the instructor calling him a very very rude name which he shouted out in an extremely loud and upper-crust accent to describe the man's effort. This informal discipline worked, the man's timing and judgement never left him again (except, perhaps, when he was having a run ashore).

The training facilities at Achnacarry were unique for their time and have since been copied in some form or another by the military authorities of most other nations.

The content of the course included such subjects as close order drill, physical training, unarmed combat, advanced weapon training, bayonet drill, boatwork, assault courses, speed marching, field craft, map reading and night patrolling; after which the trainees were expected to 'bull' their weapons and equipment up to peacetime ceremonial standards.

Once the individual element of the training had been satisfactorily completed, officers rejoined their men to carry out troop exercises. The change in the physical and mental approach of the trainees was well-known to the Depot staff. In the first week the men were dead-beat physically, morale was at its lowest point and many felt like giving up. In the second week things started to come together and the trainees were not so ready to give up. By the third week the physical exertions were beginning to pay off, morale was good and all thoughts of giving up had been erased from their minds. The fourth week saw the trainees in superb physical condition, their morale was excellent, every man experienced a high sense of accomplishment. The catalyst which brought about this change was the unrelenting pressure of the course. Achnacarry had offered a unique challenge. The men who seized upon this challenge and successfully completed the course had achieved an undreamed level of military prowess, self-confidence and fitness.

Individual features and obstacles became legendary:

The mock graves at the entrance to the castle; the wordy tombstones detailing in what way a man had not put into practice what he had been taught;

The Toggle Bridge: every Commando soldier carried a toggle rope, a piece of one inch line looped at one end with a wooden toggle spliced into the other end. Joined together these ropes could be used to construct a rope bridge and if properly made could support the weight of up to six men. Tarzan films come to mind as a similiar bridge was usually seen but made from jungle vines. They were precarious to cross under ideal conditions and the instructors were witness to feats of involuntary acrobatics, unheard of in a gymnasium. At Achnacarry the trainees invariably crossed this bridge with thunder-flashes and live ammunition exploding beneath them. Ironically, the site of the bridge was just yards from the permanant iron foot-bridge which crossed the river. Accidents inevitably occured and on one occasion two men were killed when they fell from the bridge into the fast flowing river below and were swept to their deaths.

The Death Ride (Slide): this heart stopping idea was the brain child of a Cameron Highlanders officer, Alick Cowieson, who saw the need for a way of crossing an obstacle quickly, in this case the fast flowing River Arkaig. A rope was secured from the top of a tree on the near bank of the river and to the bottom of a tree on the far bank. The distance between the trees was approximately 50 feet, the height between 30 and 40 feet above the river. Using a toggle rope looped over the slide a man could descend down to the other bank at a rapid rate of knots. As the inventor found out to his cost, the secret was to ensure that the rope forming the slide was pulled very taunt; any slackness resulted in the rope sagging with the man ending up in the river. To hurry the men along it was quite normal for the descent to be made whilst live ammunition was exploding in the river below.

Tarzan Course: a series of rope swings, single rope bridges and grappling nets, designed to instil confidence of heights was devised by one of the Staff SNCO's, CQMS Frickleton. It was constructed amid the topmost branches of a line of beech trees, believed to have been planted in 1745. The length of the course ran for approximately 50 yards with the different combinations of swings and bridges changing every 15 to 20 feet. The heights varied between 30 and 40 feet above the ground.

Abseil Descent: the mountaineering technique of abseiling was taught, using the vertical walls of Achnacarry House for the initial training sessions. Abseiling required a strong nerve and complete faith in the equipment. The trainees were instructed in this skilful art by people who ridiculed the thought of using gloves and rigorously ensured that no man ever wore two pairs of trousers. During the early stages of training ropeburns on the hands, groin and buttocks were commonplace.

The most spectactular feature of the training was the Night Opposed Landing Exercise, which was always the finale to the course. The exercise was carried out in as near battle conditions as it was possible to create without the casualties that such a landing would produce in actual warfare. As in other phases of the training where live ammunition was used, casualties inevitably occurred.

The object was to land raiding troops (the trainees) on to a defended beach, from which they would be faced by a barrage of live ammunition fired by the instructors, who were past masters at 'shooting to miss.' Small arms, machine-guns firing on fixed lines, mortars, smoke canisters, stun grenades, thunder-flashes, verey lights and parachute flares were all used to simulate the defensive opposition likely to be encountered in battle conditions. As the commandos came ashore from their boats live grenades would be exploding in the shallow muddy water. After they had placed their demolition charges against the target they would withdraw under fire. Whilst paddling away from the beach in the assault boats, it was quite likely that mortar bombs would drop so close to the boats that the occupants would be soaked in the spray and live rounds fired from Bren guns would hit the hand held paddles of the men who were propelling the retreating craft away from the beach.

One of the finest tributes ever paid to Charlie Vaughan and his staff was by Colonel Bill Darby, Commanding Officer of the American 1st Ranger Battalion, whose men had trained at the Depot. His unit had successfully carried out a hazardous and difficult operation during the Italian Campaign and when asked by a very high ranking American officer what had been the single most important part of the training before the operation he replied, 'Whatever the Rangers have achieved is entirely due to the training received at Achnacarry.' Many Commandos and Rangers left Achnacarry remembering two things above all else,

1) the instructors chant of 'It's all in the mind and the heart,'and

2) it always rains at Achnacarry!

Approximately 25,000 personnel passed through Achnacarry, soldiers and Royal Marines from Britain, servicemen from the United States, France, Belgium, Holland, Poland and Norway. The extensive use of live ammunition, together with the nature of the countryside and the man-made obstacles that the trainees had to cope with resulted in 40 men being killed during training; of which 44 unfortunately had its share.

After the war, Achnacarry House and the estate was handed back to

Colonel Donald Cameron (son of Lochiel) and all traces of Commando training were removed.

The Achnacarry Experience
7th September–2nd October 1943

Achnacarry lived up to its reputation when 44 detrained on their arrival: it was raining! Like all units the Commando formed up and marched the seven miles from Spean Bridge to the Depot accompanied by the pipe band. For the front ranks marching immediately behind the pipers, they had the sight of an incredibly bandy bass drummer marching to their front. The fact that he was wearing a kilt emphasised his gait and at least some of the 'bootnecks' arrived at Achnacarry with a smile on their faces. After arriving, the remainder of the day was spent settling into the camp routine.

During the first week of training it rained on five days and A Troop suffered the first casualties on the Assault Course, with more to come from within the other troops of the unit. Lt A.Martin was the first officer casualty when he twisted his ankle 'rope-swinging,' he was closely followed by Capt Farquarhson-Roberts, who broke his ankle and was removed to Onich Hospital. The most common injuries throughout the unit involved the knees and ankles.

One five mile and two seven mile speed marches were completed in reasonable times. The five miler was completed in times ranging between 43-53 minutes with approximately 8% of the unit failing to complete the course in the alloted time. On the seven mile march S Troop had the first man home in 61 minutes and there were very few failures.

44, alas, suffered its first major casualty when a marine in A Troop lost his left hand whilst training with a Type 69^2 grenade which also injured the officer instructor. Although in deep shock, the injured 'bootneck' gave orders to his colleaques 'Try and find my ring lads!'

The first week was rounded off with an ENSA show which the CO and his officers attended on the Saturday night.

The second week started with a seven mile speed march with times of under one hour being clocked by many officers and marines. Later in the week two nine mile speed marches were completed in good style

---

2   The Type 69 'Bakerlite' grenade was fitted with an instantaneous fuse, the detonator being operated by a ball bearing. This grenade delivered a mild stun explosion and was used fairly indiscriminately during training exercises.

by all ranks. Although five officers completed the march with times of around 75 minutes, Mne Ferguson (S Troop) recorded a time of 71 minutes.

Major General R.G. Sturges, CB, DSO, RM, made a two day visit to the Depot during which time he met all of 44's officers. The depot pipe band beat retreat in his honour and the marines were issued with oil-lamps for use in their tents. Minor injuries were being sustained and among the officers Capt Winter and Lts Martin, Hughes, Barrett and Owen all received injuries to legs and feet. Lt Dexter joined the unit from the RM Holding Commando and took up post with S Troop.

Rain, sometimes very heavy fell on every day but one during the second week of training. On 19th September Sgt E.H.Gibson and Cpl A.Dooley (C Troop) were killed whilst they were operating a 2" mortar during a live firing exercise. This accident was probably caused by an unstable mortar bomb amongst the rounds being used at the time.

Things began to look up at the start of the third week, the first two days were dry! The rain came later and continued for the remainder of the week. The officers endured two cross-country marches on and around Ben Nevis and they also completed a 12 mile speed march, 12 officers finishing in times of one hour and 50 minutes. The end of the week signalled the completion of the Individual Training phase of the course and two officers, two SNCOs and 119 marines were discharged to other units within the Corps.

In the fourth and final week the Commando commenced the Troop Training segment of the course. On 29th September A, B, C and HQ Troops completed the 30 mile cross country march whilst D, X and S Troops carried out the Strong Point and Opposed Landing exercise. On the following day the roles were reversed and 44 lost another man killed when Mne Farrell died as a result of an accident which took place during the Strong Point exercise.

The weather naturally remained wet throughout the final week. Before 44 left the Depot three more officers left and in the resulting shake-up Capt P.S.B.Baxter assumed command of A Troop. Having completed the course 44 began the journey south to Folkestone, in two trains, leaving Achnacarry in the late afternoon of 2nd October 1943.

Thirty-three Officers and 532 marines had reported to Achnacarry for training. At the completion of the Commando course the unit had lost approximately 125 officers and marines who had either been injured or been considered as unsuitable by the training staff. When 44 left the Depot its establishment stood at 28 officers and 411 marines.

Folkestone
3rd October-12th November 1943

When the Commando arrived at Folkestone the whole unit lived out. The landladies of the town provided accommodation for the officers and marines who had been split into ad hoc groups depending on the size of the accommodation on offer, 'terms' being arranged locally. Such was the discipline and ésprit de corps instilled into the Commandos at Achnacarry that the men were almost always billeted in civilian properties and not in barracks or camps when returning from Scotland. This policy underlined the requirements of initiative, ingenuity and self-discipline that every commando soldier was expected to meet. Once the unit had settled in at Folkestone, the marines continued with a strenuous training programme, the object of which was to maintain the high standard of individual, sub-section, section and troop training with at least one full Commando exercise being carried out. In general, the marines concentrated on speed marching seven or nine miles on alternate weeks, the norm being to march one mile in ten minutes. The men carried both personal and troop weapons plus ammunition for all arms, returning as a formed body ready for action. A period of close-order drill was usually conducted immediately the speed march finished. A 12 mile march on hard roads was carried out weekly with a 25 mile cross-country march being completed every two weeks.

Physical training was based on the Achnacarry syllabus (including log drills) and undertaken by all ranks every second day. In addition to individual fitness routines, much emphasis was placed on weapon training, six hours per week being devoted to the subject in addition to the time spent on the ranges.

The unit also carried out boat-training on the South Coast beaches; ranging from manning small 'collapsibles' to loading/unloading heavy weapons and Jeeps from landing craft. Promotions were made in the junior ranks and the Commando was reinforced later with the arrival of a further six officers and 67 other ranks.

The days at Folkestone slipped by. S, X and HQ Tps supplied men for church parades at the Royal Marines Depot at Deal. The RM Depot dance band provided the music at the unit Dance held at the Leas Cliff Pavilion.

Things turned serious on 2nd November when 44 were issued and fitted with new tropical kit. 'If it touched, it fitted,' was the order of the day and it was rumoured that the issue of this kit was a ruse to fool enemy spies as to the Commando's destination. However, Royal[3] was not keen to be seen wearing an Australian-type slouch hat and bush shirt, for the green beret had been hard won at Achnacarry. The usual dental checks, innoculations/vaccinations were given to all ranks and more ominously all indications as to the unit were erased from the mens paybooks, kitbags and the Quartermaster's boxes and panniers.

On 10th November an advance party left Folkestone to join HMT *Reina del Pacifico* in Liverpool. The next day all the Commando's officers travelled to Deal to attend a lecture, the subject... the Far East.

Everything indicated that 44's destination was to be India. This was confirmed when the unit reached Liverpool. A docker told the marines:

(a) the ship's destination,

(b) the length of the time the voyage would take; and

(c) the identity of the other military units aboard.

This breach of the usual secrecy which surrounded such information was discovered by the unit's Security Officer, Capt Sturges, and the ship once loaded, remained alongside the quay for another two days.

Back at Folkestone the landladies' bills were settled and some insisted on giving their 'lodgers' a farewell drink. In one house the marines were subjected to the good news/bad news treatment. Each marine was given a tot of whisky (not all that easy to obtain in wartime Britain) which was good; the bad news was that the landladies in question insisted that the whisky was drowned in milk!

In the late evening of 12th November, 44 left Folkestone station in two trains for Liverpool. All the usual scenes of wartime departures were witnessed. Men saying goodbye to wives and sweethearts amid tears and best wishes, while NCOs were trying to account for all their charges. More than one man was 'well-oiled' by the time the trains were ready to leave and many games of hide and seek were played with the NCOs. One game was to board the train from the platform, immediately open the carriage door trackside, jump down onto the railway lines before jumping back up onto the platform for another round. Those in charge were not amused.

The Special Service Group

The decisions taken in 1943 to create more Commando units had far-reaching consequences for the future organisation and structure of

---

3   Royal - affectionate nickname for Royal Marines.

Winston Churchill's brainchild. Since 1940 all Commando forces had been administered by the Special Service Brigade, which at one time directed eleven separate Commandos. With the creation and training of all the additional units it became apparent that a full-scale reorganisation was warranted to co-ordinate the work of the commando forces.

The Special Service Group was formed in October 1943 and commanded by Major General R.G.Sturges KBE, CB, DSO, a Royal Marines officer who appointed Brigadier J.F.Durnford-Slater DSO, formerly a gunner to be his deputy. The group would have under its command four Special Service Brigades, each of which would contain four Commandos, led by an officer of brigadier rank. The intention was to form separate Army and Royal Marine Brigades. The Royal Marines were to be committed to the Normandy landings with the Army Commandos being used in all other theatres of war overseas.

The new organisation experienced a very shaky start to its existence. It was recognised that inter-service rivalry between soldier and marine would create problems that, if not nipped in the bud, would be detrimental to both branches of the armed forces. In the Mediterranean, both Army and Royal Marine Commandos had fought together in shared operations, working well in each other's company. Maj Gen Sturges and his staff identified shortcomings in the original organisational structure and saw the opportunity, based on the Mediterranean experience to weld the two services together. For that reason, Special Service Brigades of mixed Army and Royal Marine units were created.

The choice of 'Special Service' as the formations title, which when abbreviated became 'SS,' bore an obvious comparision with the sometimes notorious German SS Storm-troopers. In December 1944 the title Commando was substituted for Special Service and applied to all four Brigades, who from then on were known as Commando Brigades.

After 44 had finished training in 1943 the unit joined No's. 1 and 5 Army Commandos and No. 42 (RM) Commando to form No. 3 Special Service Brigade, commanded by a Royal Marines officer, Brigadier W.I.Nonweiler.

Why the Far East?

The decision to send a Special Service Brigade to the Far East was made in the late summer of 1943. Lord Louis Mountbatten, Supreme Allied Commander, South East Asia, had made the case for three Commando Brigades to be allocated to his command. The Special Service Group could not hope to fulfil this request due to the large number of Commando units needed for the Normandy landings that were planned to take place in less than 12 months time. It seemed likely that 1 Special Service Brigade would be earmarked for the move East, but following further considerations which took into account the Brigade's previous active service engagements, the number of experienced men and specialists i.e., cliff-climbers and canoeists within that Brigade, it was felt that 1 Special Service Brigade could be used more profitably in Europe.

On 30th September 1943 the decision was made to send 3 Special Service Brigade to Burma. Unfortunately, the Achnacarry syllabus had not covered jungle warfare, tropical heat, disease and leeches. If the marines thought that they had been exposed to rain in Scotland it was nothing compared to the monsoon weather experienced once they reached the Far East.

When Major General Orde Wingate of Chindit fame became aware that a Special Service Brigade was being sent to Burma he made representations to the War Office to the effect that it should be allocated to his command.

At Combined Operations Headquarters there was a certain amount of agreement with Wingate's view and the hierarchy felt that Wingate would like the exceptionally fit Commandos, understand their specialist role and, most importantly, the Brigade would receive jungle training from Chindits who had experience of long- range jungle penetration operations. A senior officer was sent from Combined Operations HQ to India to discuss with Wingate the Brigade's future role.

The briefing note carried by this officer was clear on a number of points:

1) The Brigade would require extensive jungle training.

2) The Brigade could not be considered a permanent part of Maj Gen Wingate's Command.

3) The Brigade must always be made available to carry out amphibious landing operations should the need arise.

This preliminary planning was to be of no avail as Maj Gen Wingate was killed three months after the Brigade arrived in India and the Chindits' operations ceased shortly afterwards.

Sea Time I
The Voyage to India
15th November-19th December 1943.

44 Commando arrived in Liverpool during the forenoon of 13th
November and immediately embarked aboard HMT *Reina del Pacifico*
together with 5 Commando and several hundred other military
personnel bound for India. There were a large number of
servicewomen, mainly Wrens and nurses on board, which necessitated
an adjustment of the usual messing arrangements. Subalterns used the
senior rates' accommodation, including the ship's chapel; even this
tranquil quarter of the vessel had been commandeered to provide
messing accommodation. The displaced SNCOs messed with the
marines. Once on board, both Commandos settled in and had their first
meal. Not only was the ship very crowded but it was also 'Dry.'

The *Reina del Pacifico* had been taken up from trade by the Admiralty
at the start of hostilities. Owned by the Pacific Steam Navigation Co.,
the ship was a medium-sized (17,700 tons), twin-funnelled passenger
liner built in 1931. The diesel engines which powered the four
propellers produced a service speed of 18 knots. The ship was an
impressive looking vessel and until the outbreak of war had been
engaged on a regular service, sailing between Liverpool/Callao (Peru)
and was commonly known as 'The Queen of the Pacific.'

The ship's interior splendour was altered somewhat when being
converted to undertake troop transport duties. One obvious area to
suffer was the catering. The galleys were inadequate to cope with the
increased numbers of people on board and complaints concerning the
variety, quality and quantity of the meals were received by 44's officers
throughout the voyage. Not all the marines were unhappy about the
food, some were more worried that essential items stocked in the Dry
Canteen were in short supply towards the end of the passage East.

The responsibility for messing rested with the Ministry of War
Transport who in turn delegated the responsibility to the owners of the
vessel. Troop officers had little chance of changing things for the better
as would normally have been the case when they received complaints.

The *'Reina Del'* left Liverpool at 1400 hours on 15th November to sail
in convoy to India, which came as no surprise to 44's marines. The ship
became part of Convoy KMF 26 which proceded north escorted by the
cruiser HMS *Birmingham* and six destroyers. The North Atlantic in
November was, as usual, cold and windy with a moderate sea running.

The two Commandos received a training priority over all other units
on board. Due to the limited upper deck space available, the two units
used the training area in rotation. Boots and anklets were worn by all

ranks every day up until noon, full battle-order was worn four times per week in an effort to acclimatize the men to the hot conditions to come. In the afternoons the messdecks were used as a venue to hold lectures, when all personnel received instruction on such things as the Japanese Army, India, health in the tropics, jungle warfare, escape and evasion as well as the normal military training. The mess-decks were cramped and dismal, with the smell of body odour and vomit hanging in the stale air; definitely not the ideal surroundings in which to give and receive instruction. The ship's evaporators were over stretched to the point where the available fresh water supply was used strictly for drinking and cooking. Everyone on board quickly realized that the manufacturers' claims in relation to the sea-water soap used when taking a salt water bath or shower was so much bunkum; it was impossible to obtain a decent lather to soap one's body. Early in the voyage, with the portholes and dead-lights shut tight, the mess decks were claustrophobic, especially to those men slow to gain their sea-legs. Once the ship reached warmer climates the troopdecks became unbearably hot.

The canvas wind shutes rigged to direct fresh air down into the interior of the vessel had little or no effect in relieving stifling conditions below decks. Due to the conditions, lectures rarely lasted more than 30 minutes without a break. As a consequence of the special training requirements of the Commandos the usual fatigue parties which were provided by most of the other units on board were kept to a bare minimum.

The decision to mix Army and Royal Marine Commandos was well founded. The marines of 44 benefited from the close association forged with 5 on the ship which lasted throughout the Burma campaign.

5 Commando, raised in July 1940 had already been in action on Madagascar and their demolition teams had gone ashore during the Commando raid on St Nazaire. Their officers passed on much valuable information to 44, especially on specialist training matters and administration, the Royal Marine officers welcoming the information exchanges with their counterparts in 5. The Army Commando officers invariably stressed the reasons behind orders and instructions given to the junior ranks, anticipating the likely return questions that would be asked. The soldiers' healthy awareness of their individual responsibilities both to their immediate comrades and to the unit were also seen and digested by 44's officers.

As the voyage progressed 5 and 44 began to dominate the sporting events that took place on board. Probably due to 5's soldiers being taller and heavier than 44's marines and having amongst their ranks more experienced boxers, the Army Commandos gained more honours. However, the camaraderie never flagged between the two units.

After the convoy changed course, first to the south-west, then south the weather began to moderate.

The officers kept themselves occupied by playing a vigorous game which involved a medicine ball, a rope, and much huffing and puffing! A week after leaving Liverpool the weather conditions were such that a concert was held on the aft well-deck.

At 1100 hours on 24th November the first Action Stations was sounded. The embarked troops crowding the upper decks were ordered to their respective accommodation below and donned life jackets to await whatever was to come next. On this occasion the alarm proved to be false, but events later in the voyage justified the decision that all troops should be below decks during air raids. Later in the day HM Submarine *Stonehenge* joined the convoy. In the early evening it was possible to see the coast of Morocco on the starboard bow as the convoy turned to enter the Strait of Gibraltar. During the night the convoy passed the 'Rock' and the cruiser HMS *Coventry* joined the escort during the dark hours.

25th November saw the convoy in the Mediterranean. The popular belief that it was always sunny in that part of the world was quickly dispelled, the weather was very cloudy with a fresh wind blowing. During the afternoon a number of ships joined the convoy from Oran (Algeria); HMS *Birmingham*, flagship of the escort screen since the convoy had sailed from England, departed. With the additional ships from Oran, convoy KMF 26 now numbered 24 ships, steaming in six parallel columns at 13 knots with an escort of one anti-aircraft cruiser and six destroyers.

Air Attack, 26th November 1943

The day dawned bright and clear, the sea state was moderate with a long swell, and the ships continued to steam east towards the Suez Canal, passing Algiers during the morning. The convoy held a course which ran parallel to the North African coast, approximately 15 miles from the shoreline.

The enemy successfully jammed the escort ships' radar equipment and the first indication that the convoy was about to be attacked was when German aircraft were sighted at 1640 hours. The attackers comprised a mixed force of 20 Heinkel HE177 and Dornier DO217 bombers, escorted by six unidentifed fighters. These aircraft circled around the ships in pairs for 20 minutes, out of range of the convoy's anti-aircraft barrage. The convoy maintaining course and speed was about to be assailed by a new and potentially deadly enemy weapon, 'the glider bomb.'

The Henschal HS-293 glider bomb was probably the world's first guided missile. A miniature aircraft with a wingspan of ten feet, it carried a 1100lbs warhead in the nose. It was carried to within range of its target by a parent aircraft and once released a rocket motor powered the bomb to reach a speed of 370mph in 12 seconds.

When the missile reached its optimum speed the motor cut out, the bomb continuing in a shallow gliding dive towards its objective as the parent aircraft turned away. It was understandable that this new weapon was easily mistaken for an enemy aircraft. Those missing their targets crashed into the sea, being claimed (by various ships) as aircraft destroyed. The lasting impression of those who saw these bombs was either of a crimson ball, or sparks and flames being emitted from the rear of the bomb. The missiles actually carried a bright flare, enabling the aimer in the parent aircraft to guide the bomb, by means of a radio signal, towards the intended target.

The first attack was launched at 1700 hours, directed towards the escort vessels on the port side of the convoy. Four near misses (within 50 feet) were recorded, one each to HMS *Coventry*, two destroyers and one merchant vessel. The bomb aimed at *Coventry* hit the sea directly alongside the ship. When the bomb exploded, the cruiser heeled over to such an extent that it seemed doubtful, to those who saw the incident, that the ship would right herself.

She was lost from view in a mountain of spray, *Coventry* appeared through the screen of foam, still rolling furiously as she drew clear and unharmed from the maelstrom which the exploding bomb had created.

The second attack occurred at 1730 hours following the same general pattern as the first strike but with two major differences! Several enemy aircraft launched torpedoes, all of which missed the intended targets, and, secondly, a glider bomb struck a vessel with fatal consequences. HMT *Rohna* (8,600 tons) had joined the convoy the previous day, being one of the ships that had sailed out from Oran. She was transporting 2000 American servicemen to Port Said. In addition to the troops, the vessel also carried a crew of 218 officers and ratings.

The missile which hit *Rohna* was released from a DO217, being clearly visible for between five and ten seconds before it struck the target. It was observed to be gliding on a horizontal plane between ten and 15 feet above sea level. The bomb pierced the ship's side before exploding in the engine room. To those on board the explosion did not sound very loud; observers on other ships noted the amount of red flame, smoke, and debris that was thrown into the air. It was estimated that fragments including an abnormal amount of paper, reached a height of 200 feet above the stricken vessel. The engine room caught fire and began to fill with water bringing about a complete loss of all electrical power. The top mainmast collapsed and fell forwards; the bulkhead separating the engine room from the troop deck gave way and the ship began to list to starboard. The Captain immediately gave the order to abandon ship. Of the 22 lifeboats carried, six were smashed by the explosion and some jammed in their davits. Troops prematurely cut the falls of several of the other boats which toppled into the water and rapidly became waterlogged. Only eight boats were successfully launched, most of which capsized or filled with water in the fairly heavy seaswell that was running at the time.

Unlike the British, the American troops had not cleared the upper decks when the convoy was attacked. It is probable that several hundred troops standing on the open decks were killed when the glider bomb exploded directly below where they had congregated. Most of the surviving troops and crew jumped from the ship using life rafts, hatch-covers and anything else available to keep afloat. HM Destroyer *Atherstone* together with a US minesweeper began to pick up the survivors under cover of a smokescreen. As darkness fell the task was not made any easier as the lifejackets worn by the troops were not equipped with red survival lights. Of the 2,200 men on board *Rohna*, approximately half that number were rescued from the sea and landed on the North African coast. With the collapse of the internal bulkheads the fire and flooding soon spread to the aft holds and 90 minutes after being hit the ship sank by the stern.

During the air attacks on the convoy, a British flotilla of seven LCI.(L)s [Landing Craft Infantry (Large)] was passing KMF26, sailing in the opposite direction on a course which took them between the convoy and the coast. The landing craft were on passage to Algiers from Djidelli to embark troops. These ships also engaged the attacking enemy aircraft when in range, claiming one aircraft shot down.

The crews on the landing craft could clearly see the burning *Rohna*, which had fallen behind the convoy; the vessel was an estimated 15 miles from the flotilla's position. However, the Flotilla Commander chose not to send any of the vessels under command to give assistance. This incredible lack of judgement, once it was brought to the notice of the C-in-C Mediterranean, resulted in this officer, (an acting lieutenant commander, RNVR) being relieved of command. Subsequently, the 'acting' rank was withdrawn and, reverting to his substantive rank of lieutenant he was reassigned to the General Service Branch of the Royal Navy.

No other ships were hit during the air raid and the 'all clear' sounded at 1840 hours. The enemy's use of the glider bomb had been an unexpected development in the style of air attack. Although these weapons would be relatively ineffectual against armoured warships, they could be devastating when used against unprotected merchant shipping. With a range of three miles, the bombs were launched beyond the range of anti-aircraft fire. The missiles needed to be destroyed as they closed on the target. The troops on board the 'Reina Del' hurriedly mounted eight Brenguns along either side of the vessel as a counter-measure to the new threat.

The following two days were uneventful. The general low cloud cover and rain prevented the expected air raids, Cape Bon fell astern and HM Submarine *Stonehenge* left the convoy during the dark hours.

Air Attack, 29th November 1943

KMF26 continued to steam eastward at a steady 13 knots, the coast in sight at intervals for most of the day. At 1420 hours the convoy was attacked by 16 Junkers JU 99 bombers escorted by six fighters. The aircraft approached from the south-west, flying over the convoy at 2000 feet. They were met by a concerted barrage of fire, including 44's Brenguns mounted on deck. The attack was not pressed home with any determination by the German aircrew whose aim was deterred by the heavy flak put up by the convoy's anti-aircraft guns. The aircraft made one diagonal pass across the convoy to drop their load, before disappearing to the north-east. There were several near misses, one bomb hit the fo'csle of HMT *Ranchi*, passed through the side of the ship, killing one man, before exploding in the sea along the vessel. The damage to this vessel (transporting 1 and 42 (RM) Commandos) led to *Ranchi* remaining in Alexandria for repairs. The two Commandos did not join the Brigade in the Far East until January 1944. Several enemy aircraft were hit during the action which proved to be the last air attack on the convoy.

The two days between the last air action and the ships arriving at the Suez Canal were fine and hot. The only ongoing problem affected the tug-of-war competition held on deck. The teams pulling towards the stern gained a definite advantage with the slope of the deck in their favour!

On 2nd December the 'Reina Del' entered the Suez Canal without the usual stop at Port Said, which robbed the marines of the chance to sample the delights of this cultural oasis. Instead, the ship anchored in the Bitter Lakes overnight before continuing its passage through the canal to Suez, travelling on through the Gulf of Suez and into the Red Sea towards Aden. During the day a concert party was organised and a concert held the same evening.

The ship sailed independently, the troops on board undergoing the introduction to very hot weather. At night the temperature below decks inevitably reached the high 90's and at least 25% of each mess were permitted to sleep on deck. This part of the voyage was more relaxed; mess-deck portholes were open all day and in addition to the canvas wind chutes, various wind scoops were fitted to the portholes in an effort to divert the sea breeze into the troop decks. Smoking was permitted on the upper decks and recreation/sports events were organized; including the first bouts in the open boxing tournament.

The 'Reina Del' arrived at Aden at 0830 hours on 8th December, remaining at anchor in the harbour for five days until joining a convoy bound for India. The period spent anchored off Aden was uncomfortable due to the very hot conditions, especially below decks.

The CO requested permission to land his marines to carry out military exercises, the request was rejected for 'security reasons.' Exercise was confined to dancing to the music of an RAF dance band which went on board to provide the accompaniment for an all ranks dance held on deck.

The convoy sailed from Aden at 0700 hours on 13th December in company with, amongst others, the fleet repair ship HMS *Resource* and the fighter direction ship HMS *Boxer*. Other vessels in company carried landing craft, which was of interest to the amphibious-trained commandos. The Royal Navy provided five escort vessels. During the seven-day voyage across the Arabian Sea the convoy was joined by the aircraft carrier HMS *Battler* (the converted US merchant vessel *Mormacmail*) whose aircraft provided a continuous anti-submarine air patrol over the convoy for the remainder of the passsage. As HMS *Battler* joined the convoy so HMT *Arundel Castle* detached. This ship had accompanied the 'Reina Del' since leaving Liverpool.

The sporting competitions were completed, 5 Troop, 5 Commando won the tug-of-war competition and 44's Sgt Smith won his bout in the finals of the boxing tournament.

Before the ship reached India all organised training came to an end. Steel helmets were stowed away in kitbags and all English money was handed in for exchange. On 19th December the coast of the Indian subcontinent was sighted during the forenoon and, at about the same time, an aircraft from HMS *Battler* ditched into the sea, fortunately the aircrew were picked up by one of the escorting ships.

The *Reina del Pacifico* docked alongside the quay in Bombay at 1500 hours, 34 days after leaving Liverpool. Orders were received that 5 and 44 would disembark at 0700 hours on the following morning. Before 3 Special Service Brigade went ashore they received a visit from their commander, Brigadier W.I.Nonweiler.

2
India

After the ship docked, 44's marines had wiled away the afternoon and evening (19th December) savouring the atmosphere of India and watching the native dockers begin to unload the vessel. The Indian stevedores worked at a frenetic pace amid a scene of apparent chaos. The general hustle and bustle on the quay, the incomprehensible shouting and gesticulations of those in charge were observed by the embarked troops with a wry amusement. India was obviously going to provide an eye opening experience to the majority of the marines on board.

Reveille was sounded on board the *'Reina Del'* at 0445 hours, the troops, having breakfasted, disembarking promptly at 0700 hours. Both units boarded trains for the journey to Kedgaon. From the railway station the marines were ferried to the camp by road. The last sections of the Commando arrived in darkness. Some weeks later the entire Special Service Brigade came together with the arrival of 1 and 42 Commandos following their stay in Alexandria. Each of the four Commandos passed comment on the camp thus:

> 1 Commando: 'A bare rocky dusty plateau whose only recommendation as a camp was unlimited space.'

> 5 Commando: 'A tented camp with a remarkable bareness of outlook.'

> 42 Commando: 'Were not impressed with the camp but it was memorable for the amount of football played there.'

> 44 Commando: 'A cold, windswept, bleak and bare hill, mottled with large black rocks. An occasional tent and bamboo building stood in the wilderness. The word 'Kedgaon' should be used to describe acres and acres of nothing.'

The initial days in camp were spent on improving the very basic amenities, the major priority being the fumigation of the bug infested beds, cleaning the field kitchens (galleys) and latrines (heads).

Christmas was coming. On Christmas Eve the marines were paid, the

• DEHLI

ASSAM

• ALLAHABAD

② SILCHAR

SIRAJGANI
MYMENSINGH

①

② CHITTAGONG

B
U
R
M
A

CALCUTTA

COX'S
BAZAAR

I N D I A

AKYAB •

• NASIK
BOMBAY
• AHMADNAGAR
• POONA
• KEDGAON
KHARAKVASLA

②

WALTAIR

• COCANADA

• BELGUAM

BAY OF BENGAL

②

BANGALORE ②

MADRAS
JALARPET JUNCTION

CALICUT ③

④

KARUR

TRICHINOPOLY

④

③

DHANUSHKODI

④

TRINCOMALEE

INDIAN
OCEAN

③

③

MAYO

COLOMBO •

• KANDY

CEYLON

REFERENCES TO INDIAN
CITIES/TOWNS IN TEXT
n.b. Place Names pre-1947

→ RAIL JOURNEY

① AKYAB - SILCHAR

② SILCHAR - BANGALORE

③ BANGALORE - TRINCOMALEE

④ TRINCOMALEE - MADRAS

showers were available for use every other day and, in keeping with the season, midnight mass was celebrated by the Catholic padre. For many of the marines this was their first Christmas spent abroad. The usual Christmas fare was served. Dinner was eaten in the open-air during which time 44's officers took over all guard duties. Each man was issued with three bottles of beer and the day was rounded off with a traditional evening carol service.

The days between Christmas and New Year were spent on improving the condition of the camp. By 1st January 1944 the camp was almost 'Pusser.' The galley was still short of cooking utensils and the water supply was spasmodic. However, the camp was in far better condition than when 44 had arrived. Working parties were utilised to prepare 42 Commando's tent lines in readiness for their arrival. An assault course was built: approximately one thousand yards in length with 12 obstacles. The marines would wear full battle order and carry personal weapons to run the course in a maximum time of seven minutes. A small 30 yard small arms range was also constructed.

HQ Troop. The Commando Brigade's rig of the day out East was invariably 'bare buff' as it helped reduce the occurrence of prickly heat. Note: 30% of the men still favour the slouch hat.

Training continued non-stop. A three week 'commando course' was set up to provide specialist training for the reinforcements who had not been through Achnacarry before joining 44. Lt Rider was designated chief instructor. Lt Col Horton ensured that his men became acclimatised to the tropical conditions and every opportunity was taken to harden the feet. The early training was mainly centred around speed marching and long cross country route marches, with a strong emphasis being placed on water discipline. The training programme was intensified with night exercises being carried out at troop and unit level. Time was spent on boat training and landings, plus practical sessions in discovering how to live off the land.

A visiting jungle team spent three days with 44. The officers and SNCOs received detailed lectures and practical demonstrations on the art of jungle fighting. Many useful tips and hints were digested, despite the countryside surrounding the camp being the exact opposite of that needed for jungle training. The lack of a suitable jungle training area was noted and commented upon by a visiting Australian officer, Brigadier Lloyd, who had had experience of fighting the Japanese in the jungles of New Guinea.

With jungle warfare in mind the marines were issued with jungle green battledress. The slouch hats issued in Folkestone were to be worn with a green puggaree: the Combined Operations badge to be affixed on the left, with the Corps badge showing to the front. What started as a very formal type of headgear did not survive for long. Sometime later an instruction was promulgated stating that 'Bush-hats can be worn in any manner to suit the wearers taste.' The result of this order was that both officers and marines fashioned the head-wear into many different shapes and styles. In any case, the marines always preferred to wear the hard won green beret, and the bush hats were eventually discarded. 'To suit the wearers taste' was taken by 'Royal' to extend to haircuts! Although the regulation 'short back and sides' was kept, some hairstyles were outlandish. Parts of the head were shaved to leave all manner of hair patterns growing under the marines' berets.

The Special Service Brigade attracted some very notable military visitors: on Boxing Day, 44 received a visit from the Commander, 29th Infantry Division, Major General F.W.Festing DSO. As 44 were temporarily attached to 33 Indian Corps, the GOC, Lieutenant General M.G.N.Stopford CB, DSO, MC. made a formal inspection of the camp on 4th January, D Tp provided the Guard of Honour. Following the arrival of 1 and 42(RM) Commandos on 21st January, Brigadier W.I.Nonweiler visited his unified Brigade on the 22nd January.

The round of official visits and inspections was completed in some style on 23rd January by Admiral Lord Louis Mountbatten, the Supreme Allied Commander, South-East Asia Command (SACSEA). He ordered the marines to break ranks and 'gather round.' Some officers and SNCOs looked less than pleased. After the most detailed preparation to ensure a smart formal turnout, the immaculate ranks of men on parade were fallen out! The Supreme Commander addressed 44 for ten minutes, the theme in the early days of his appointment being based on the three M's: monsoon, malaria and morale. Lord Louis was blessed with the capability of raising morale almost instantly. He exploded the myth that the Japanese soldier could not be defeated in the jungle. The assembled marines were told that most Japanese were city dwellers; and short-sighted city dwellers at that! Later Admiral Mountbatten was introduced to the Commando's officers, the youngest marines and men awarded medals from previous campaigns. He won the hearts and minds of 'Royal' by directing that a day's holiday be given to all ranks.

The JNCOs opened their club, beer went on sale in the canteen, the marines were entertained by Indian conjurers in the camp area and they also learned not to trust the wildlife. A group of bootnecks left the galley holding mess tins loaded with soya link sausages; everyone oblivious to the dangers lurking above. High in the sky a large hawk picked its target, zeroing in on the meal held by a marine renowned for his appetite. The bird gathered speed in the silent headlong dive towards its goal. With a deftness honed over thousands of years, the final approach, snatch and accelerating climb with the soya links held in vice like claws was a beautiful sight to behold. As his comrades collapsed in an hysterical heap, eyes blinded with tears of laughter, the marine in question had, in turn been: startled, flabbergasted, decidedly annoyed and left bereft of a marine's usual sense of humour.

On the more formal side, 44's officers mess held a mess dinner for the officers of the other Commando units and Brigade HQ. Not to be outdone the SNCOs held a social evening with an invitation being extended to Brigadier Nonweiler, the commanding officers, officers and SNCOs of the rest of the Brigade.

The officers' ranks were strengthened with the arrival of a further two lieutenants, plus 21 marines. Capt Hamlin, Lt Macan and three SNCOs were temporarily detached to a front line Army unit to gain first hand experience of jungle fighting, returning to 44 five weeks later.

In early February, Lt Col Horton outlined to his SNCOs the unit's future anticipated moves. All leave was stopped and the Commando left Kedgaon on 20th February in company with 5 and advanced Brigade HQ. The troops marched to the local railway staion and entrained for an overnight journey to Bombay and destination unknown.

Sea Time II
Bombay-Cox's Bazaar
22nd February-4th March 1944

The marines arrived in Bombay in the early afternoon of 21st February. The embarkation of the two Commandos and Advanced Brigade HQ, plus the loading of stores and equipment, went on throughout the evening and into the early hours of the following morning.

HMS *Keren* (ex-British India Steam Navigation Co. vessel *Kenya*) was the marines introduction to the Landing Ship Infantry (Large). The ship was taken-up from trade by the Admiralty at the beginning of World War Two being converted to carry troops and landing craft. A ship of 14,200 tons, the twin screws powered by steam turbine engines produced a service speed of 17 knots. *Keren* carried a total of 14 assault landing craft of various types, with deck space to accommodate 30 15-cwt trucks. The ship's company numbered 210 officers and ratings, with quarters for 80 officers and 1218 other ranks on the troop decks. The armament included one 6" and one 3" naval guns, ten Oerlikon anti-aircraft guns on single mounts and, surprisingly, three depth-charges!

The ship moved into the harbour at 0815 hours and set sail, in convoy, at midday. Lt Col Horton addressed the Commando, telling the marines the destination of the Brigade: Chittagong! The convoy would sail down the west coast of India, around Ceylon (Sri Lanka) and across the Bay of Bengal to reach the port. The marines quickly settled down to the ship's routine. At sea the Commandos of both units carried out general maintenance of weapons, small arms training and played deck hockey.

The convoy steamed south reaching Madras on 27th February. *Keren* dropped anchor in the harbour, awaiting a berth at the fuel oil jetty. With the ship at anchor, 5's Concert Party put on an impromtu concert, much to the glee of the remainder of the Brigade. When the ships sailed on 29th February, two additional troopships had joined the convoy. Once at sea, the marines were assembled to be told that the Brigade's destination had been altered. The Commando would be landed at Cox's Bazaar,[4] a small port south of Chittagong, close to the Burmese border.

Keren arrived off Cox's Bazaar on 4th March., the Commando being

---

4   Cox's Bazaar was named after a British Officer (Lieutenant Cox) in 1799. Lt Cox created a settlement on the Indian coastline on being appointed to oversee the movement of Arakanese refugees seeking sanctuary across the border in British territory after escaping from the invading Burmese.

ferried ashore in the ship's landing craft. 'Royal' was greeted on the beach by the native population: the local people had prepared enormous bathtubs full of sweet tea which the marines gratefully accepted. The unit spent the night in a rest camp before moving off on the following morning.

Nhila
5th-10th March 1944

Nhila, situated halfway down the Teknaf Peninsula on the River Naf, was the advance base from where 44 would depart to make its first operational amphibious landing. The days were occupied with making final preparations for the forthcoming action and troop leaders received their final orders/instructions. During this period, Capt Hamlin, Lt Macan and the three SNCOs returned to the unit from their detached duties with the Army. On 10th March Brigadier Nonweiler visited the Commando, speaking to all ranks before they boarded local river craft for the short trip to St Martin's Island.

Swimming off St Martin's Island

Lying off the coast of Burma opposite the coastal village of Alethangyaw, the island would in peacetime be described as a tropical paradise. 'Royal' took the opportunity to swim and sunbathe during the afternoon. Lt Col Horton addressed the Commando in the evening and found his marines in fine form. 44 was ready for action!

The Second Arakan Campaign, the Allies advance south into Burma through the Arakan region, a stretch of jungle-clad hills separating central Burma from the Bay of Bengal, commenced in December 1943. The plan almost came to grief when the Japanese mounted an offensive just days before the planned Allied attack began. Vicious jungle fighting ensued. For the first time Japanese jungle tactics were defeated and a full scale onslaught was repelled by the Allied forces.

B Troop checking the route to Alethangyaw

Unloading stores at St Martin's Island

The Brigade's role entailed supporting the Allied offensive to capture the Maungdaw/Bulhidaung Road, vital to the 14th Army (Lt Gen W.Slim) plan to push south. The sparse port facilities at Maungdaw were needed to enable General Slim to receive seaborne stores and equipment. The ultimate goal was to continue the advance south to reach Akyab.

The Jungle

The tropical jungles of the Far East presented the most arduous, unpleasant, unrelenting and cruel environment in which to wage war. Jungle fighting required nerve, patience and reserves of physical stamina. Every man involved in movement through this, the most difficult of all terrains, required the mental ability to overcome the feeling of claustrophobia induced by the lush, overhanging and often impenetrable growth on the jungle floor. The dense green foliage was usually dripping wet and rotting vegetation released a stomach churning stench when disturbed. The degree of daylight that penetrated through the canopy of trees, some of which rose 80 feet towards the sky, was extremely limited. At ground level what little light there was cast deep shadows. It was possible for a soldier, suitably camouflaged and remaining stock still, to be within arms length of his enemy and remain undetected.

During the dark hours the speed of advance was severely hindered by the pitch black conditions. In heavy jungle the field of night vision was reduced to one or two feet and contact was maintained by every man clutching the bayonet scabbard of the man in front. In these conditions each man felt almost alone, only aware of those others immediately to his front and rear in the column of march. The dense jungle surroundings played havoc with one's sense of direction and almost completely erased the ability to hear any background noise. Often the only human sound heard was that made by the man himself or those very close to him. The speed at which plant life grew to blanket paths created by passing troops was startling. Within twelve hours, all signs of human intrusion was obliterated by the rapid growth of the jungle.

The humid conditions were not immediately obvious; the canopy of trees created an impression of shade, giving to the uninitiated, the expectation of cool surroundings. However, the steamy heat was ever present and within a short space of time every man would be saturated in sweat, clothing clinging to the body.

The webbing straps of the men's equipment would begin to chaff the

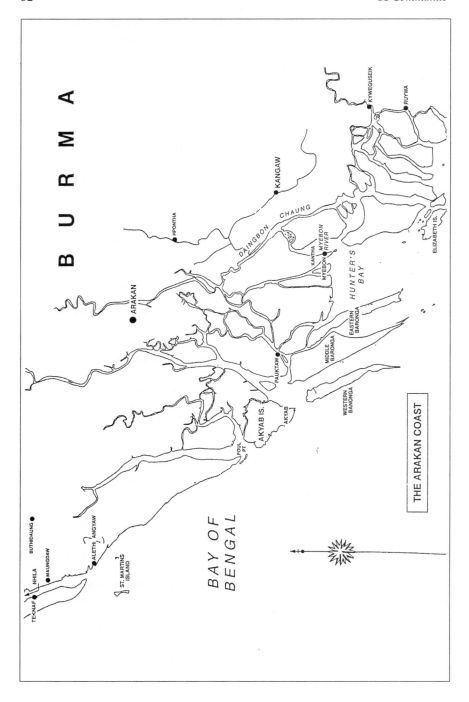

THE ARAKAN COAST

skin, gently at first before inexorably blistering or rubbing the skin raw. Ether way the jungle filth would enter the wound and rapidly turn the injury septic.

Watercourses usually covered a bed of sticky black mud and were the natural habitat of the leech. This disgusting blood sucking worm was a constant companion on any jungle patrol. It has a mouth centred in the front sucker. Indeed some species have small teeth. The leech lives as a parasite, sucking on the blood of other animals or humans for nourishment. They can be either red, brown or black. Some may have stripes or spots on a body which can expand up to eight inches in length. The marines became hardened to the sight of several of these bloated insects, several inches long, clinging to the skin. Leeches were found in large numbers near swamps and streams. They also clung to grass stems which necessitated clearing long grass from the vicinity of sleeping areas. An automatic body inspection was carried out at each halt. The only way to prevent the insect attaching itself was to keep the body covered. Spare boot-laces tied around the ankles of trousers prevented leeches crawling up the legs, although they had a nasty habit of crawling through the lace holes of a man's boot. At night the ears were plugged with cotton wool as a preventative measure.

The leech, once attached to the body required to be removed without leaving the blood sucking fangs in the flesh. Burning off with a cigarette or the application of salt were the usual methods adopted; the worm being sensitive to heat and drying. On one occasion a marine suffered more than most from leech wounds: he bled continuously for ten hours.

The hostile environment posed the problem of having to deal with jungle fevers, mould and foot rot. Men displaying symptoms of fever were subjected to treatment based on the old adage of being 'cruel to be kind.' Under normal circumstances, any man showing signs of contracting a fever was given two mepacrine tablets and made to march on, carrying both his weapons and equipment. The fever was usually sweated out of the body within a few hours. The frailty of the human body, not used to the incessant strength-sapping heat and humidity reacted in different ways. It was quite possible for a man to sleep in the jungle and awaken to discover a foul-smelling mould developing in the areas of the crotch or armpits. From time immemorial the bane of any infantryman's life has always been foot rot. The jungle conditions in Burma exacerbated the problem. The sweltering, dank surroundings made it impossible to keep the feet dry. An especially severe form of foot decay was suffered by the jungle fighters. Akin to the more common Athletes Foot, extremely large painful open cracks appeared between the toes; the surrounding skin exuding a smell of decaying flesh.

The jungle was always alive with animal noises which reached a crescendo at dawn and dusk. The clumsy movement of troops often scared creatures off; the sudden loud exodus of monkeys and birds, followed by a deathly silence was certain to warn the enemy of an approaching column of troops.

The time and effort expended to hack through thick undergrowth with machetes resulted in speed of movement being dramatically reduced. It was soon appreciated that, in the jungle, usually accepted map calculations bore no relation to the ground actually covered. Distance was always measured in hours marched. All movement made along jungle tracks was made in single file and without the benefit of flank protection. The density of the jungle terrain prevented standard European military tactics being employed.

The strenuous nature of jungle patrolling dictated that the minimum of equipment be borne. In addition to personal weapons and ammunition, each man carried a small pack. This usually contained four days rations, soap and towel, paper, string, a clasp knife, half mess tin and spoon, cellophane bags containing cigarettes and matches, mepacrine tablets, sterilization tablets, cotton wool, salt and local currency (one Indian rupee notes); the money being useful to purchase local produce from the native population. On occasions when the usual 'K' rations were not available, food provided for a ten man patrol consisted of tinned bacon and cheese, bread (one loaf per man), packets of biscuits, nuts and raisins, tea and sugar. The rations carried were augmented by local purchases from friendly natives. The combination proved to be adequate, but by no means ample, all fresh food having to be eaten within 24 hours.

The consumption of drinking water was strictly controlled. At rest halts, taking fluids prior to resuming the march, as opposed to reaching for the water bottle immediately a halt was called, resulted in a saving of the supply carried. Any water taken from fast flowing sources required to be purified with sterilizing tablets. The bottom sections of bamboo trees occasionally yielded an unexpected supply of water. When cut near the base, some trees contained a small amount of clear water, suitable to use as a mouth rinse. With water supplies always presenting a problem, an additional water container, the 'chugal' (a slightly porous canvas container, not dissimilar to a domestic hot water bottle) was issued to every second man. When filled, water seeped through the canvas sides and evaporated, this having a cooling effect on the contents. The chugal provided a surprisingly effective method of carrying the precious water supplies.

Not surprisingly, sweat rags were regarded as an essential item. The standard gas cape combined with the mosquito face veil provided a greater degree of protection against flying insects than the stock issue mosquito net. Medical supplies, iodine, calamine and field dressings to treat and dress wounds inflicted by the jungle and its creatures, were essential.

Experience highlighted the necessity to select rest areas some distance away from streams and tracks leading to water. Any source of water was a breeding ground for mosquitos and leeches. Well-trampled paths indicated that they were often used by wild animals; including elephants!

3

The Arakan

Operation Screwdriver I
2330hrs 11th March-0800hrs 15th March 1944

44(RM) Commando carried out its first operation in classic Commando style. A landing from the sea, a move inland to harass the enemy, followed by an ordered withdrawal back to the beach and subsequent re-embarkation.

Once ashore 44's task was to neutralise the enemy in and around the village of Alethangyaw. The Commando would move into the surrounding hills from where the marines would be in a position to contain the Japanese in the area, preventing enemy reinforcements from using roads leading north and jungle tracks east. The Allies main attack on the Maungdaw/Buthidaung road commenced at 0500 hours, 12th March, north of 44's position. If the operation went as planned, the retreating Japanese would come under attack from the positions held by 44.

The tried and tested 'Box' defence (a rough square, with piquets posted at each corner protecting, for example, the Commando HQ set in the centre), would be established during the daylight hours. The Commando would march at night to change position thus misleading the enemy as to the location of the main force.

11th March, the landing:

The amphibious landing took place at 2330 hours from LCPs[5] in three waves. The operational order laid out the troop assignments as follows:

1st wave A & D Troops to clear the area around Alethangyaw. 2nd wave C Troop to act as immediate reserve and to mop up any enemy resistance in the village; B Troop (minus one section) to provide local protection to the heavy weapons of S Troop; S Troop; HQ.

---

5   Landing Craft Personnel: Length 25', beam 6' and constructed of plywood, these
     craft could carry at least 18 men. A single Chrysler engine gave the craft a top
     speed of 12 knots. With no landing ramp fitted, these vessels were designed to
     carry the 'second wave' troops to the beach.

3rd wave X Troop, Commando reserve; B Troop (one section) to provide local protection to the demolitions team.

Naval support was provided by a motor launch and four landing craft support vessels. The Commando's first operational landing was unopposed. However, a good many men were totally immersed in the heavy surf running at the time.

The initial attack:

A and D Tps 'pincer' attack (C Tp as immediate reserve) on Alethangyaw in the darkness soon developed into a confused battle in and around the village. It was apparent to the marines that the village was defended far more strongly than anticipated at the planning stage of the operation. Advancing on the village, A and D Tps came under sniper attack from the rear, the marksmen hidden in the treetops. The unit's progress was also held up by fire from light machine guns until the enemy positions were eventually cleared by B Tp using small arms and grenades.

At an early stage of the attack, Commando HQ made contact with A Tp (Capt Baxter) located on the western side of the village who had dispersed into a shallow depression. A Tp had run up against the most strongly defended area of the village. Any movement drew fire from enemy light machine guns concealed in areas on either flank of the marine's positions. Commando HQ was unable to confirm the position of D Tp (Capt Winter), although Capt Baxter reported that elements of D Tp were to the east and south of the village market place.

It was clearly obvious to Lt Col Horton that the initial attack was becoming bogged down. Although enemy sniper fire was unnerving and control difficult, the CO observed that much of the fire was both erratic and inaccurate. He ordered D Tp to move to the north of the village and C Tp (Capt K.Martin) to pass through A Tp to 'mop-up' in the village. Although hindered by sniper fire, C Tp continued the move towards the objective until being pinned-down by fire coming from an enclosed compound.

As C Tp advanced to the northern side of the village, one section (Lt Musters) lost contact with the remainder of his Troop as did a section of D Tp (Lt White). During this phase of the attack the 2i/c (Maj Macafee), was wounded and evacuated to the regimental aid post set up on the landing beach. The prolonged and confused fighting against a well concealed enemy continued. The marines fought running battles between flimsy huts built from dried vegetable matting stretched between bamboo poles and topped with a thatched palm leaf roof; all the huts proved to be very combustible. It was becoming obvious that

44 would not be able to clear the village and move on into the hills before daylight as planned.

12th March:

The CO informed the Brigade Commander of the current position, the marines being forced to 'box' around their existing positions before dawn. From first light the Commandos were subjected to continuous sniper attack and fire from light machine guns. During the day several lone Japanese soldiers infiltrated the box defence before being killed. In the afternoon casualties were inflicted on enemy forces withdrawing from Kanyindan. After being subjected to almost continuous sniper fire since landing, 44 went on the offensive, the unit's own marksmen targeting enemy soldiers still occupying Alethangyaw village market place. During the day 44 witnessed at first hand Japanese inhuman treatment of prisoners. A patrol (2/Lt Mackinnon) was directed to reconnoitre the proposed route to be taken by 44 during the forthcoming night move into the hills. The patrol was ambushed, 2/Lt Mackinnon and one marine receiving serious wounds. The officer managed to crawl into nearby cover where he was found by his own men and evacuated. The marine was found by the Japanese and although shot in the head, he was still alive. His seemingly dead body was dragged into the open and covered by enemy machine guns. The marine was left exposed, without medical attention, for three days. Any attempt to rescue the man by his own comrades would have proved fatal. Once the Japanese had withdrawn, the marine, miraculously still alive, was carried to safety by local natives. He was subsequently repatriated to the UK where he made a full recovery.

The move into the hills:

Before moving, the casualties sustained during the day were evacuated to the north through 81st West African Reconnaissance Regiment's lines. The attached personel of 55th Observation Squadron set deception devices in the Commando's lines, some timed to actuate eight hours after 44 had cleared the location. Prior to the Commando moving out, enemy mortar bombs began to bracket 44's positions. The move north-east towards the foothills began immediately it became dark (1930 hours). The Commando crossed the Taungdo chaung (chaung: Burmese term for a tidal river or large stream) without difficulty. The leading elements reached the foothills shortly after moonrise, unseen by the enemy. At times the impenetrable tangle of vegetation forced the marines to divert to the chaung and wade through the chest-high water for long stretches. In the almost pitch dark, the conditions made movement intermittent and contact between men difficult. Orders were relayed along the line of marines in whispers and over a period of time all elements of the unit became thoroughly intermingled. At the first halt the positions of A Tp HQ plus one section, C Tp leader with one section and D Tp HQ plus one section could not be established.

13th March:

The advance continued until 0330 hours. The noise of movement as men stumbled through the dense bamboo vegetation made the occupation of the highest surrounding features impractical. The Commando therefore formed its box on lower ground before dawn broke. A piquet was left at the chaung to guide the rear file of marines to 44's main position. At daybreak sentries were placed on the highest accessible points. Before settling down for the day, the Commando had the satisfaction of hearing the Japanese softening up 44's recently vacated positions. The marines heard the unmistakable sounds of heavy mortar fire, a sure indication that the enemy were preparing to launch a large-scale attack on the positions they had recently vacated.

Operations in the Hills:

The day started ominously with the accidental discharge of a No.4 Lee-Enfield rifle.[6] The chaplain, Rev H.C.W.Manger RNVR, received mortal wounds; Lt Col Horton and the adjutant (Capt Parish) received superficial injuries.

During the day a fighting patrol (Capt Hamlin) was despatched to reconnoitre a junction of two tracks and attempt to locate the missing sections commanded by Lts White and Musters. The enemy were using

---

6   During World War Two, many modifications were made to the Lee-Enfield rifle. Small engineering companies, employed to produce component parts altered the original designs. One such alteration was the omission of the half bent from the cocking piece. This change produced a rifle positively dangerous to use. The experiment was short-lived and the half bent was restored. It is probable that this rifle was one of a faulty batch made during this period.

the tracks and the distinctive imprints of Japanese jungle boots were easily recognised. The patrol returned without either engaging the enemy or coming across the missing sections. Other patrols sent out came into contact with opposing forces and inflicted several casualties without loss.

Radio contact was eventually made with Capt Baxter following hours of silence. He had under command sub-sections of A and C Tps. This group had established an excellent observation post high above the area north of the chaung. The marines were able to observe both the road and known enemy held positions in the area. Japanese signallers broke into the unit radio net however and shortly afterwards, Capt Baxter's observation post was located and attacked. Casualties were inflicted on the Japanese with no losses to the defenders. The radio link was re-established between Commando HQ and the vessel carrying the Advanced Brigade HQ after a break of 21 hours.

The afternoon brought good and bad tidings: D Tp HQ and one section, detached during the previous night's march, rejoined the Commando. However, it appeared that 44's position had been pinpointed by enemy patrols. An attack was expected at any moment. Again the marines prepared to move out of the Commando box under the cover of darkness. Before moving, the chaplain was evacuated by stretcher, the demolition detachment providing the stretcher bearers and escort for the journey. At 1945 hours the Commando vacated its position in darkness and moved north through particularly wet, dank and difficult jungle country. Dripping with sweat, soaked from wading through numerous small chaungs, clothing and equipment saturated, the marines slogged on, stumbling over unseen hazards on the jungle floor. In addition to the obvious physical discomforts, the mental strain imposed in staying alert to the possibility of the enemy springing an ambush, fully stretched 'Royals' body and soul. To compound the already adverse conditions being experienced, every man was subjected to enduring the attentions of the extremely irritating mosquito fly.

14th March:

A halt was called shortly after midnight. After forming the protective box, by now an automatic drill, 44 rested until daylight. During the day two fighting patrols were sent out. One patrol commanded by Capt Hamlin laid an ambush at a well-used track junction. No contact was made with the enemy. Capt Sturges' patrol engaged the enemy on several occasions, inflicting several casualties without loss. Later in the day Lt Col Horton received orders to prepare to withdraw to the coast. 5 Commando was to land and take over 44's role the next day.

The Withdrawal:

The Commando began to move out from its box at 1715 hours. After successfully using deception devices at Alethangyaw, further ploys and deception tactics were set-up around the vacated positions to mislead the enemy.

The detached group under Capt Baxter was ordered to rejoin the Commando. This proved to be easier said that done: the Japanese had already attacked the observation position forcing the marines to fight a running battle throughout the entire journey back to rejoin the unit. The skirmishing continued until the Japanese came under fire from the main body of the Commando. Gunfire indicated that the group's recently cleared positions were being attacked in strength. The Commando, now reformed, awaited moonrise before moving off again out of the hills.

15th March:

44 moved off shortly after midnight towards the coastal plain. Lt Col Horton faced the dilemma of having to choose one of two routes. It was obvious that the Japanese were fully aware of 44's existence, but not of the unit's exact location or intended movements. The Commando moved back over familiar ground and the CO accepted the risk that the chaung offered an ideal position in which the enemy could lay an ambush. In the event this proved to be a well-chosen route. The forward elements were almost clear of the hills before the marines in the van attracted any enemy opposition. A single enemy machine gun opened fire which was light and ineffectual, allowing B and X Tps plus Commando HQ to reach the plain unscathed. A second machine gun began firing at the same time as a grenade attack was launched, initially pinning down the Commandos still in the jungle. The fire from the two machine guns was unco-ordinated and the waiting marines reached the plain some 20 minutes after the attack began. Once on the plain 44 moved rapidly across country to pass through the 81st West African Reconnaissance Regiment outposts without further contact with the enemy. With the exception of the guides sent to establish contact with 5, the two units did not meet. The Commando reached Cypress Point at 0800 hours and re-embarked onto landing craft for the journey back to Nhila. The degree of strain that the operation had imposed on the men only became apparent when the unit reached the beach for re-embarkation. The unit had been on the move virtually non-stop; they were soaked through, unkempt and tired.

The tiring nature and physical isolation of jungle fighting resulted in individuals only being aware of their immediate involvement; many men were completely oblivious to much of what had gone on. The marines' level of fitness, however, was such that all personnel had fully recuperated within the space of 24 hours.

The first operation against an opposition renowned for its use of the jungle taught the marines invaluable lessons. Most of the known Japanese's tactics were encountered:

> -snipers in trees, shooting after a file of men had passed below;

> -using wounded comrades as bait to inflict further casualties;

> -calling out in English, tempting the marines to reveal their positions;

> -breaking into the unit's radio net to pass misleading messages. It was rumoured that the C.O. had, on one occasion during the operation, unwittingly spoken to an enemy operator.

This first experience of fighting the Japanese indicated that the feared reputation was, to a degree, undeserved. The early estimation of the Japanese soldier depicted a fanatically disciplined individual, meticulous in performing his duties and a supremely able jungle fighter. The equipment he carried was functional: his weapons, however, were often inferior to those carried by Allied troops. Two different rifles were issued: the model 99 rifle fired 7.7mm: whilst the earlier (1905) rifle fired 6.5mm rounds. The magazine capacity of both weapons was five rounds as opposed to the British Lee-Enfield's ten. Model 99 ammunition could not be used with the Japanese standard issue machine gun, unlike the interchangable .303" Lee-Enfield rifle/Brengun rounds. The marines met with an incredible amount of inaccurate fire. Where enemy weapons were found, the ordnance was both dirty and ill-maintained.

The attacks on 44's vacated positions indicated poor intelligence. Most telling was the enemy's apparent inability to lay ambushes in country which was eminently suitable for such action. If 44 had been surprised whilst wading through the chaung, the marines would have sustained a high number of casualties.

The CO's concern was that his men, basing their judgement on experience gained during the operation, did not begin to underestimate the prowess of the Japanese soldier.

Movement through the thick jungle for the first time brought about large groups of men losing physical contact with the main body of the unit. In the main, this was largely due to the inexperience of both officers and SNCOs in leading men in jungle country, especially at night. It also reflected the lack of jungle training. Although Achnacarry was probably the finest training centre in the world at the time, no-one could have created the type of close country in which the Commandos operated when fighting in South-East Asia.

44 returning from Operation Screwdriver

The number of casualties inflicted on the enemy was conservatively estimated at between 35 and 50 killed, with an unknown number wounded. 44's losses were two officers died of wounds and two wounded; two other ranks missing believed killed, 11 wounded, two missing (5 Commando later found the body of one marine and two Japanese around a prepared position at Alethangyaw.

This operation marked the Royal Marines' first land action in the region since the marines of Viper Force (a unit of four officers and 104 marines manning motor launches providing coastal patrols) left Burma in May 1942 during the great retreat North. During the evacuation of Rangoon they were the last troops to leave, forming a river patrol to cover General Slim's Burma Corps retreat up the Irrawaddy.

Returning from Operation Screwdriver

The Missing Sections:

One section of C Tp (Lt Musters) became detached during the initial advance from the beach towards Alethangyaw village. The marines came under fire from light machine guns positioned to the north of the heavily defended market place. During this confused point in the early fighting, the section lost contact with the remainder of its troop. Lt Musters was guided back to the main beach by local natives, digging in to await low tide. Later, they moved along the beach until reaching the 81st West African positions. The Alethangyaw chaung was crossed enabling the party to reach the bridgehead at Dodan. Their numbers were swelled by Lt Carryer with ten marines from X Tp, together with a sub section of D Tp, who had been escorting and carrying early casualties back to the West African lines. The total of 44 personnel gathered together numbered around 50. This detachment assisted in the defence of the area until it rejoined the unit at Cypress Point prior to embarkation.

Lt Rider and Capt Sturges in warlike pose

One section of D Tp (Lt White) moved through Alethangyaw from the west during the initial stages of the operation. The marines encountered resistance coming from a heavily fortified bungalow and although the building was protected by wire, an assault was made on the position. During the attack Lt White was wounded and a SNCO killed. The Japanese were occupying a very strong emplacement and the marines, under heavy continuous fire from well concealed positions, were compelled to withdraw. Unable to contact the remainder of D Tp, the section moved in the hills independently, happening on other members of the troop who had become detached from the main force. The augmented section later succeeded in locating the 81st West African Division and gave their assistance in the local defence of the area until able to rejoin 44 at Cypress Point.

A sub-section of A Tp (Lt Owen) lost contact with the unit on D+2 after crossing a chaung during the night move north. After a brief reconnaissance Lt Owen moved his men to the summit of the nearest accessible hill to await daylight. During this move to high ground Lt Owen, a SNCO and a marine made an unsuccessful attempt to locate the remainder of the troop. This small party ran into a sizeable Japanese patrol. The marines' Tommy guns jammed during the ensuing firefight and, after throwing grenades Lt Owen's team melted into the jungle. The sub-section then succeeded in contacting Capt Baxter (A Tp leader) by radio to report their position. Lt Owen sent a small patrol out to meet Capt Hamlin's men, who were known to be in the vicinity. The position of 44's box was passed to Lt Owen and his detachment was able to rejoin the main unit without further incident.

Marine Bill Nutt carves 'another notch on the rifle butt'

Nhila
15th-21st March 1944

On the return to Nhila, the marines were met by Colonel R.F.Cornwall, MBE[7] (SEAC Headquarters), who came to visit his old unit. After 'Royal' had received an issue of rum, tea or both, all weapons were

---

7   When a lieutenant colonel, this officer had commanded the 3rd Battalion, Royal Marines. Many men in 44 remembered Col Cornwall from those days. His black muzzled features had inspired the all too obvious lower deck nickname.

cleaned and every man took the opportunity to shave for the first time since leaving St Martin's Island six days earlier. The time spent at Nhila was used to catch up with both personal and unit administration. Weapons were serviced, transfers/promotions promulgated and the unit received a visit from the public relations men.

Lt Col Horton addressed his marines, speaking of the lessons learned during this first encounter with the enemy. He also speculated on the likely involvement of the Commando in future operations in the area. The CO together with Col Cornwall made a brief visit to the Maungdaw front line. When the two officers returned, the men were given notice of the unit's imminent return to operations.

On the 20th March, the CO led an advance party of marines drawn from all the rifle troops to take up positions at Nahkaungdo (quickly christened No-Can-Do by 'Royal'). The following day the Commando was given a hearty breakfast before boarding local river steamers for a three hour passage to join the advance party at Nahkaungdo, where they arrived at mid-day.

Operation Screwdriver II
1200hrs 21st March-1100hrs 12th April 1944

While the Commando rested at Nhila, operations against the Japanese continued, the progress of 'Screwdriver' being pursued with interest. After landing to relieve the marines, 5 were relocated to take over the 81st West African Reconnaissance Regiment's positions, continuing the policy of harassing the enemy. During this phase 5 Commando were ambushed by the Japanese. Two rifle troops were sent out from Maungdaw to provide protection to a battery of field-guns in danger of being overrun. The Army Commandos fell victim to a surprise attack, becoming trapped as they moved through a very narrow pass. The soldiers extricated themselves after a prolonged battle in which they were pinned down for several hours by enemy machine guns. During the action 5 lost 27 men killed. Lt Col Horton had on previous occasions emphasised to his marines the distinct possibility of being ambushed in the jungle terrain. 5's misfortune came as a timely reminder to 44 that the Japanese soldier should not be underestimated.

44's second assignment was initially to relieve 5 and subsequently operate in front of the 9th Indian Infantry Brigade. The Royal Navy were no longer able to supply the land forces from the original landing beach, all stores and manpower being transported through Nahkaungdo by landing craft. Ashore, the marines' duty was to patrol the surrounding terrain collecting intelligence data on Japanese

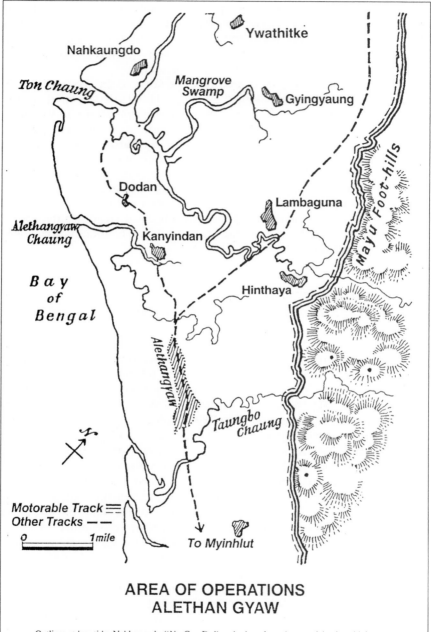

Nahkaungdo

Ywathitke

Ton Chaung

Mangrove
Swamp

Gyingyaung

Dodan

Lambaguna

*Alethangyaw
Chaung*

Kanyindan

B a y
of
B e n g a l

Hinthaya

Alethangyaw

Mayu Foot-hills

*Taungbo
Chaung*

Motorable Track
Other Tracks
0   1 mile

To Myinhlut

AREA OF OPERATIONS
ALETHAN GYAW

Outlines at low tide. Nahkaungdo ('No-Can-Do') and other places become islands at high water.

strengths, unit identifications, enemy movements. Where possible patrols were also tasked with registering the topography of the area.

The initial 3 Special Service Brigade order to Lt Col Horton indicated that 44's rifle troops would broadly hold the positions occupied by 5 Commando:

Commando HQ and A Troop	Nahkaungdo
X Troop	Kanyindan
B and S Troop	Dodan
C Troop	Lambaguna
D Troop	Ywathitke

The CO identified certain weaknesses with these dispositions:

-Ton chaung could only be crossed on foot at low tide.

-The only dry means of crossing the chaung was by way of a very basic, narrow footbridge at Lambaguna.

-During the operation to date, sampans had proved to be the best form of water transport available. However, these vessels were only available in limited numbers, were slow and dependent on the river currents.

-In most cases the local craft were manned by untrained native crews.

Lt Col Horton felt uncomfortable with the fact that, if these weaknesses were exploited, the positions at Kanyindan and Dodan were likely to be cut off. To protect these villages, the proposed offensive patrolling would become, by definition, defensive. By leaving these areas unoccupied, additional manpower would be available to reinforce the area around the strategically important Lambaguna bridge, the crossing needed if operations were to be carried out on the southern side of the chaung. The force of argument was overwelming and the CO was granted permission to amend the planned disposition of his men as circumstances dictated.

An advance party of 50 marines, led by Lt Col Horton, carried out an initial reconnaissance of the positions held by 5 Commando. The first thing noted was the level of the chaung at low water, any craft using the chaung would become stranded in thick mud during this phase of the tide cycle.

The timing of the exchange between the two units would be critical. If they arrived close to low tide, the exposed mud would severely hinder the movement of men, stores and equipment between the sampans and banks of the chaung. The two commanding officers (Lt Col Horton and Lt Col D.M.Shaw MC) discussed the exchange. 44's CO received the unpleasant news that local intelligence reports indicated that an estimated 400 enemy troops occupied Alethangyaw village. The likelihood of enemy troops launching a night attack on the Commando's positions at Dodan and Kanyindan, to coincide with 5's departure, presented a genuine threat. To counter any disruption at the changeover, the marines' advance party was immediately dispatched to both locations to cover 5's withdrawal. Both Commandos stood to arms throughout the night, awaiting the expected assault. For whatever reason, the attack did not materialise. At first light the withdrawal from both villages commenced. The marines retired with their army colleaques, leaving the positions unoccupied as planned. The time taken to cross the chaung to reach the two villages convinced Lt Col Horton that the permanent occupation of these positions was unsound.

The change over between the two Commandos began at dawn on 21st March. The plan involved 5 Commando using all available sampans to cross the chaung to establish a defensive position to cover 44's landing at Nahkaungdo.

In the light of recent experience, Lt Col Horton revised his troop locations from the original positions laid out in the Brigade Order:

Commando HQ and A Troop	Nahkaungdo
B and C Troop	Lambaguna and the Bridge
X and S Troop	Gyingyaung
D Troop	Ywathitke

Although the attack on Dodan and Kanyindan had not developed, the threat of a large number of enemy troops in Alethangyaw needed to be addressed. As 44 approached Nahkaungdo, packed tightly together on two towed Higgins dumb barges, Allied dive-bombers flew low overhead to attack the Japanese positions. Later, when the marines landed it was discovered that Alethangyaw was unoccupied. The landing craft grounded 50 yards from the beach. Their late arrival was blamed on the falling tide. It was obvious the Inland Water Transport Command had not taken heed of the problems identified and passed on by 44's advance party.

The general shortage of adequate river craft created problems throughout the operation. Sampans were used to transport B and C Tps to Lambaguna. Meanwhile D and X Tps waded through shoulder high water to reach their positions on the far bank of the chaung. S Tp, with mortars and medium machine guns were moved in small reconnaissance boats to their location later in the evening. As darkness fell, all troops were in position and in radio contact with Commando

HQ. The first night passed without incident.

The marines had learned on the first mission that the Japanese were capable of breaking into the communications net. At 0500 hours on 22nd March an enemy voice was heard on the radio net.

The message received by 'Royal' cheered him up immensely! 'We know 44 Commando have returned, this time, however, you will not be so fortunate, as we have brought up a large number of guns to blast you out.' With that message ringing in their ears 44 Royal Marine Commando ate breakfast.

The first full day ashore was spent in settling into the respective troop positions. Liaison was established with the Royal Artillery, whose guns would give 44 close support if needed. Throughout the operation the rapid response and accuracy of the Gunners was excellent. The Japanese were very wary of the artillery support. On many occasions they rapidly dispersed after seeing the Verey flares used by the marines to bring down fire.

Men of 'V' Force, local guides and interpreters commanded by Allied officers, Major Dennis Holmes in this instance, provided outstanding intelligence reports on enemy movements and strengths. On the first day they reported approximately 70 enemy soldiers occupying the nearby village of Hinthaya and being joined by additional troops, streaming down out of the hills. Acting on this information, reinforcements were sent from Nahkaungdo to support B and C Tps who were being attacked at Lambaguna bridge. During this action local natives helped supply a Bren gun crew with ammunition as they engaged the enemy. The reinforcing detachment engaged an enemy patrol of 30 men, killing six and wounding others, with no loss to themselves. By the early hours of 23rd March the Japanese numbers in Hinthaya warranted artillery fire being directed against the village. The barrage was enough to persuade the enemy to return to the safety of the hills.

'V' Force acquainted 44 with the enemy's standard routine. The Japanese usually visited any surrounding villages in the hour before nightfall. The object was to obtain any food that was available before returning to the hills under the cover of darkness.

From the high ground it was possible to observe any movement made by the marines. To counteract this daylight observation, nearly all 44's patrol activities were carried out at night with the unit resting under cover during the day. The policy proved to be extremely successful. It became increasingly apparent that the enemy were always uncertain of the Commando's intentions which enabled the marines to send out offensive patrols as circumstances dictated.

The artillery fire was not all one way, however. The enemy, realising the strategic importance of the Lambaguna Bridge, shelled B and C Tps on 24th March. Thirteen rounds landed at one minute intervals. Under cover of the barrage, enemy infantry advanced on the marines' box before opening fire with heavy machine guns and grenades. The attack was driven off with the help of a counter-barrage, delivered with unerring accuracy within 15 minutes of the signal being sent to the battery commander. That was to be the only occasion that enemy artillery rounds proved troublesome. Although 44 were subjected to shellfire at other times, the artillery barrage was always ineffective.

Patrols fought several minor actions. 30th March: A patrol commanded by Capt Sturges ambushed an enemy patrol, killing five, wounding two others.

2nd April: A raid on Hinthaya village resulted in five enemy dead.

6th April: Capt Hamlin led a patrol from Gyingyaung to lay a classic jungle ambush. An enemy patrol was caught completely unawares, suffering 16 casualties, including eleven dead.

9th April: An S Tp machine gun caught a group of Japanese in open ground. Three enemy soldiers were killed, with three wounded.

Patrols, searching the surrounding hills for likely targets, often had the opportunity to bring down Allied artillery fire on enemy positions. Other patrol activities included searching for a Japanese rest camp which was thought to include a brothel; many Japanese divisions had 'comfort battalions' on their stength. 44's marines also destroyed the houses of a notoriously anti-British village headman, which the majority of the local population applauded with relish.

Capt Sturges led a boat patrol in an attempt to rescue an RAF pilot reportedly shot down in jungle country and in hiding. The airman's reported position was to the south of 44's area of operations, approximately 24 sea miles away. The first craft put at the disposal of the marines was manned by the Indian Navy. During the loading of stores, it became apparent to the Indian sailors that the amount of extra fuel being taken on board indicated a prolonged period away from base and probably in a hostile area. Before the marines boarded the launch, the crew cut the mooring lines and sailed off. The crew was later subject to disciplinary action brought by 25th Indian Division. This setback was overcome by pressing into service a local river craft manned by a native crew. The vessel was not equipped with either charts or nautical compass. Lt Macan was drafted on to the patrol as he had a limited experience of coastal navigation. When the vessel set sail, the only aids to navigation on board were a prismatic compass and a 1/4" Ordnance Survey map of the area. On a moonless night, the craft struck a sand bank, coming to rest in a precarious position and close to sinking. The native crew immediately abandoned ship, leaving Capt Sturges to salvage the craft before returning to base. The mission was aborted and the marines and crew lived to tell the tale.

An operation within an operation codenamed 'Snodgrass' was conducted over the period 2nd/3rd April. The object was to lure the Japanese out of the surrounding hills onto the coastal plain, where 44 could engage them in open country. The lure was C Tp. Moving off in daylight towards Alethangyaw, tempting the enemy to cut them off from the remainder of the Commando, C Tp reached the village before coming under fire from a 75mm gun. If the enemy came onto the open plain A and X Tps were waiting to attack. The Japanese, not taking the bait, manned their prepared positions and the operation was then aborted. The enemy gun was later damaged by Allied artillery fire.

Deception and Re-embarkation:

On 5th April, the Brigade Staff began to draw up the preliminary arrangements for a further exchange between 5 and 44 Commandos. On 8th April these plans were shelved due to enemy activity elsewhere. The Japanese began an offensive in the north of Burma, attempting to break through from Burma into India. If successful, the British 14th Army's railway links to the main supply bases in India would be in grave danger of being severed. The Special Service Brigade were to be hurriedly moved, together with part of XV Indian Corps, to cover the new threat. The Commandos would be based in and around the tea plantations at Silchar in Assam. Brigade HQ with 5 moved north on 9th April while 44 were placed under the command of 25th Indian Division until they were extracted from their positions and moved north to rejoin the Brigade.

44's re-embarkation at Nahkaungdo for passage to Nhila was arranged to take place over two nights, 11th/12th and 12th/13th April. It was vital that all boats reached the loading points by hightide (2345 hours) enabling the marines to embark and be clear of the area before dawn. Three DUKW's,[8] two large local rivercraft and one Higgins dumb barge were allocated to the task.

Radio deception began in the morning of 10th April, the aim being to persuade the enemy that any increased boat activity was consistent with 44 being relieved by another infantry unit. In fact 44's marines were told no different at the time. The authentic withdrawal plan was something entirely different:

---

8   DUKW: A six-wheeled amphibious truck, capable of carrying 25 men or two tons of cargo. Its speed was 50 mph on land, 5.5 knots (driven by propeller) in water. Range: 400 miles.

Example of one of the assortment of native craft used during the phased
withdrawal from Nahkaungdo, April 1944.

On the first night, one half of Commando HQ plus one section from
each rifle troop were to be withdrawn. During the following day, the
remaining marines would carry out routine operations, leaving their
positions for the second night's withdrawal as late as possible, in order
to arrive at Nahkaungdo by midnight. During the second day a strong
enemy patrol closed on 44's positions, presumably to investigate
whether they were still occupied. The patrol was driven off by the now
depleted Commando. Japanese curiosity had probably been aroused by
the first night's withdrawal. Two river craft with a Higgins dumb barge
had arrived nearly four hours late! Forced to await the next high tide,
the vessels left the following morning, loaded with marines in full view
of the enemy. Local sampans and dugout canoes were pressed into
service to ferry marines, still occupying the outlying positions, back to
Nahkaungdo. Most of these craft were unseaworthy. When a sudden
squall hit the boats, one craft capsized throwing its passengers into the
water. One marine (A Tp) was drowned. His body was recovered and
buried the following day.

During the withdrawal stage Lt Col Horton made vigorous
representations to the Inland Water Transport Command emphasizing
the necessity for the vessels to reach the designated embarkation points
on time. The CO was disturbed that the crews were insufficiently
trained to operate craft in tidal waters and had no appreciation of tide
tables or elementary navigation.

Native Dory. Alethangyaw, April 1944

The total inefficiency of these crews was unfortunately demonstrated on the second phase of the withdrawal. Once again the boats were late to arrive. The Higgins dumb barge was missing from the ragtag flotilla. The first of two large river craft broached beam-on as it approached the quayside.

A DUKW endeavouring to tow the river craft back into deep water was immobilized. The second river craft broke down as it approached the quay and was forced to anchor in midstream. The DUKWs saved the day however, and the first rivercraft was towed into deep water to rejoin its sister ship anchored off the quayside. The DUKWs were then employed to ferry the remaining marines out to the larger vessels. All 44's men were finally loaded on board various craft by 0300 hours on 13th April. The two river craft, lashed together, with only one of four engines servicable, set off up the Naf River to Nhila at a steady one-and-a-half knots!

The second phase of the operation had been very successful, over 50 casualties had been inflicted on the enemy with no loss to the Commando.

During the later stages Capt M.H.Davis, two SNCOs and two marines from 42(RM) Commando were attached to fight alongside 44.

Regrettably one of this party (A/Sgt J.Logan) was killed; he was the only battle casualty sustained during the operation. As in the first phase of Operation Screwdriver, 'Royal' experienced nothing positive to indicate that the Japanese soldier was an exceptional jungle fighter. Lt Col Horton, ever mindful of his marines impression of the enemy soldier, went to great pains to ensure that 44 did not become over confident.

During this second phase of the operation, Troop Sergeant Major G.W.Kemsley (A Tp) distinguished himself, subsequently being awarded the Military Medal for his actions at the time. On his own initiative he twice disguised himself as a native. Together with a marine, similarly disguised, the two men reconnoitred enemy positions from a distance of 50 yards, returning on each occasion with valuable information. Although serious at the time, there was a humorous side to the episode. When the two men put on their disguises - mainly burnt cork to blacken the skin - and walked away from their comrades toward the enemy positions, the marine, being naturally fair skinned and quite tall, was the most unlikely looking native ever seen.

Nhila/Dohazari
12th-15th April 1944

When the Commando was reunited at Nhila on 13th April, Lt Col Horton addressed the unit. He informed his marines of the plan to redeploy rapidly north to Silchar and explained the reasons for the secrecy surrounding the movement of men during the withdrawal from Nahkaungdo. Everyone in the Commando regretted leaving the area to the Japanese. 44 had developed a high regard for the local native population, now being left to the mercy of the enemy. The natives were very pro-British which was likely to bring about reprisals from the Japanese for the enemy were aware that the population had assisted the marines. Besides providing invaluable local information, the natives had always freely given food when asked. The marines had developed a taste for chicken and rice, the staple diet of the local people. These same people were largely responsible for tending and later returning two men back to the unit. The two, a lance corporal, RAMC and a Royal Marine were originally posted missing, believed killed on 15th March. In the fighting which took place as 44 retired at the end of the first phase of Operation Screwdriver the two men had been cut off from their comrades. Hiding in the jungle they were fed by the local population until they rejoined the unit when the Commando returned to the area.

After a short period of rest, weapon maintenance and replenishment of stores, equipment and ammunition, the unit boarded river craft for the journey to Tumbru, arriving in the early hours of 14th April. The Commando assembled on the jetty to await transport. At 0700 hours the marines climbed on board a fleet of 40 DUKWs for the journey to the railhead at Dohazari. After spending the night at the station 44 entrained for another day/night excursion. The Bengal-Assam railway to Silchar was of the single track, narrow gauge variety. Even the most widely travelled men in the unit found this agonizing journey uncomfortable. The slow and winding track took the train through Chittagong before 44 finally reached Silchar to rejoin 3 Special Service Brigade.

4

Assam

Silchar, the capital town of Assam lies on the banks of the Barak River and at the time was the Administrative Headquarters for the district. 44 were billeted in a local rest camp. The recent move was followed by the military classic; 'Hurry up and wait!' While the unit awaited further orders the marines settled down to normal camp life. The Commando paraded at 9.30 every morning. After being dismissed the marines continued with routine training. Lt Col Horton passed on relevant information regarding the object of the forthcoming operations within the unit's 680 square mile area of responsibility (comparable in size to the area inside the M25 Motorway). The unit was visited by the Brigade Commander, two troop commanders (Capts Winter and Martin) were transferred to 42(RM) Commando and Lt Macan was promoted to become C Tp leader. In the spare time available the Commandos went to the movies to see 'The Saint's Vacation,' played football and participated in an inter-troop rifle and pistol shooting competition, S Tp were victorious in both events.

The Commando was served notice that the monsoon season was fast approaching when a sudden gale sprung up during the early hours, blowing down several 'bashas.' The unit was also hit by the first cases of malaria, with eleven marines being hospitalised. Rounding off the downside to the first days spent in Assam, the marines had to respond to two air-raid warnings on the eve of relocating to new positions at Silkuri, approximately six miles to the south-west of Silchar.

The Monsoon

The word monsoon is a derivative of the Dutch word 'monssoen' used to describe the annual fierce wind and rain storms which sweep through Burma and the surrounding nations. High summer temperatures affect the levels of air pressure over land and sea to create two distinct seasons of monsoon weather. The dry North-East monsoon continues from November through to February/March. The South-West monsoon from mid-May to mid-October secures for Burma the distinction of being, during this period, the wettest country in the world. During the rainy season both the ambient air temperature and humidity soar; combining to impose physical strains on the body and stretching the marines' sense of humour to the limit. The cooks worked wonders to prepare food in the prevailing conditions, the men having to improvise to keep their meals dry on the journey from the galley to the mess tents. It came as no surprise to find a surfeit of watered down gravy covering the meal! During the season the usual rate of rainfall measures around 200 inches, representing nine-tenths of the annual total. On 5th November 1943 13 inches were recorded on one day alone. To illustrate the point; it is conceivable to shower in a monsoon rainstorm, provided one's naked body can withstand the power of the raindrops!

Prior to Lord Louis Mountbatten's arrival in South East Asia both the Allied and Japanese forces called a halt to offensive operations during the wet summer months. In his customary style Lord Louis informed South East Asia Command: 'There will be no drawing stumps this year, we will march on, fight on and fly on.' A boastful challenge taking into consideration that an advance of one mile per day during the monsoon was considered good progress. The rain reduced visibility to virtually zero, the incessant torrent forming huge lakes where none were shown, occasioning map reading to become a nightmare.

For 44's marines the physical discomforts of living in leaking tents surrounded by miniature raging rivers amid a sea of mud were borne with a feeling of resignation. To add to their woes (wearing permanently damp clothing and mouldy boots), there was the ever present likelihood of hurricane force winds uprooting every tent and basha not held firmly in place. Aside from these inconveniences the sudden great rain and wind storms toppled telegraph poles to sever communications, made roads impassable to vehicular traffic and completely transformed the natural geography of the region.

The monsoon weather which hit Silkuri coincided with 44's arrival. A severe electric storm lasting several hours caused untold misery to those caught in the deluge. The marines gritted their teeth, carrying on with the tasks in hand despite the torrential rain, the like of which was, to most, awe inspiring. Movements were made along mud covered tracks and over inadequate bridges spanning rocketing rivers. The waters in full spate carried debris, foliage, animal carcasses plus the occasional dead body to form temporary dams before being swept onwards by the weight of water backed up behind the obstruction. The rainstorms were invariably accompanied by dazzling flashes of lightning. A stroke of lightning killed a marine sentry (S Tp) when it struck the brass belt buckle of his webbing equipment as he stood guard. The funeral was held at Silchar with S Tp providing the pall bearers and firing party.

The full force of the monsoon necessitated that the Commando HQ tents be moved to higher ground. Mud, fallen trees, subsidence and flooded roads were the cause of numerous accidents: one of the unit's lorries overturned returning from a supply run and the CO, Adjutant and Padre had a narrow escape when the jeep they were travelling in ran off the road amid a shower of spray; finally setting down in a sea of mud alongside the track.

Silkuri
26th April-27th July, 1944

The task allocated to 44 was to stop Japanese infiltration along the eastern and southern approaches to Silchar including the Barak river. Two forward patrol bases were established in areas to the south (Dwarband) and west (Moniarkhal), both accessible to motor transport. From these points fighting patrols set out to locate and destroy enemy columns attempting to gain access to the Silchar Plain.

The Commando was sub-divided into three component parts:

> Silkuri: Commando HQ; C Troop (minus one section providing the guard on Brigade HQ).

> Moniarkhal patrol base: (OC Capt Sturges) A and B Troops, plus one signals section.

> Dwarband patrol base: (OC Capt Hamlin) D, X and S Troops (minus one machine gun section).

Each patrol base provided its own defence with not more than 50% of the force out on patrol at any one time. Rations and ammunition were provided daily by motor transport with the vehicles available to evacuate casualties and other medical cases back to Silkuri as necessary.

Military protocol was observed when the General Officer Commanding the local area, Major General R.P.L.Renkin CBE, MC, and Brigadier Nonweiler made an official visit to Commando HQ. The guard of honour was provided by X Tp, and S Tp paraded with heavy weapons.

In true Commando tradition D Tp gave a demonstration of toggle-rope bridge building while C Tp displayed their prowess on the death-slide. The GOC left 44 suitably impressed.

A and B Tps were the first to be deployed, the patrol base at Moniarkhal was established two days after the unit arrived at Silkuri.

The Dwarband patrol base was set up one week later, leaving Commando HQ and C Tp at Silkuri as planned. Although the main objective was to engage the enemy, early patrols gained valuable experience of movement in the jungle and generally acquainted themselves with the area.

Capt Watkins (A Tp) led the first three day patrol (2nd-5th May) into close-country, with men drawn from both A & B Tps. The party consisted of one officer, Troop Sergeant Major, a sergeant, a corporal and six marines. The patrol was split into two: the CO, TSM plus one marine forming the vanguard; the remainder making up the main body of the patrol. In the event of the vanguard coming under attack, the remainder of the patrol would provide the necessary support. Should both elements be attacked, the corporal and one marine would withdraw from contact, returning to the patrol base immediately to report the action and act as guides for a reinforcing column sent to the beleaguered patrol. As a matter of course two marines were detailed to provide protection against attack from wild animals. During the patrol two rafts, each costing one rupee were purchased. One eventually sank whilst the other was exchanged for a bunch of bananas. (This deal begs the question, was 'Royal' seen off?) The information brought back by Capt Watkins was digested and acted upon by every other patrol sent out during 44's time in the area.

Shortly after the rifle troops deployed, the whole area was lashed by an abnormally ferocious two hour storm. Tents were flattened and telegraph poles crashed down.

The marines experiencing their first monsoon thought back to the rain at Achnacarry, renowned for having more than its fair share of wet weather. The Scottish rain pattern, however, bore no comparison to the weather experienced in Assam.

Until 21st May, the operational situation remained tense. The bases established at Moniarkhal and Dwarband sent out regular patrols. Lt Owen with five marines (A Tp) completed a ten day patrol in a vain attempt to find an Allied aircraft which had reportedly crashed. The RAF later identified the wreckage found as a jettisoned fuel tank belonging to an enemy aircraft. The patrol found the local population friendly and helpful but 'money mad.' This failing made them an easy target for bribery by either side if money was offered.

A second patrol located the wreckage of an Allied Mustang fighter aircraft: the pilot was unaccounted for. On all patrols leeches were always troublesome and there was also a steady flow of personnel being hospitalised, most of them suffering from dysentery, septic sores or various strains of fever picked up in the jungle. On several occasions, a patrol, out in the jungle for several days, would be ignorant to the fact (usually due to radio defects) that the unit's security password had been changed. The terse exchanges between sentries and patrol leaders, as a tired, thirsty, wet and hungry patrol returned to the box, often contained very colourful marine language. No Japanese could have imitated these particular spoken words!

The local GOC accompanied by Brig Nonweiler, paid a visit to A and B Tps, whilst D and X Tps were visited by the Brigadier and CO. The unit also 'procured' a motor boat and began patrolling the Barak river. As the danger of the Japanese reaching the Silchar plain receded, 44 relaxed and started to play soccer again. Silchar cinema was the venue for an ENSA variety show starring Elsie and Doris Walters (Gert and Daisy).

Rain continued to fall: the wet conditions combined with the hot weather brought on another medical condition, prickly heat, a most unpleasant and uncomfortable complaint. The main deterrent was to take either frequent showers or stand out in the rain and thoroughly cover the body with carbolic soap.

June 1944

Despite the monsoon weather 44 continued to patrol their area of operations. Capt Watkins, a SNCO and one marine carried out a seven day patrol to reconnoitre the area around the river Sonai. This small reconnaissance party was accompanied by a SNCO and two constables from the Assam police. The police presence was useful. They were able to assist the marines as interpreters and to calm the fears of local villagers who tended to be frightened of the 'soldiers.' The presence of the military gave the policemen an added confidence to carry out their duties. The weather throughout was wet and once the patrol reached the hills the temperature dropped dramatically.

The motor boat used by 44 to patrol the Barak River broke down and all efforts to find a replacement craft were unsucessful: all the boats in the area were unserviceable.

The camp and Commando HQ site at Silchar were both steadily improved. Lt Henshall's demolition team blasted a new road into the camp and a sergeants' mess was built. The heavy rainstorms continued, necessitating the stores dump to be relocated onto higher ground. The monsoon wreaked havoc with the communication links between Commando HQ and the two patrol bases. The roads became impassable to vehicles. Local sampans and mules were used to ferry supplies to the rifle troops. The incessant rain could not extinguish a fire in the sergeants' mess galley caused by an unpredictable petrol cooker blowing up. The flames took a fierce hold destroying some of the weeks rations stored close by.

Two accidents occurred, resulting in Boards of Inquiry: a type 36 grenade exploded in C Tp's area, wounding one marine in the knee; in the other incident a marine, cleaning a colt pistol unfortunately shot a corporal through the foot. Both men belonged to D Tp.

Lt White, wounded during the unit's first operation at Alethangyaw, returned to the Commando. Within a week he was appointed D Tp leader. The Quartermaster, Capt Coole left the unit bound for the U.K. As he was an original 3 RM officer, he was given a rousing send off by all ranks. Lieutenants Macan and Martin were promoted to captain. Lt Owen (A Tp) moved over to C Tp to replace Lt Bleasdell who took over the role of unit Intelligence Officer.

The Commando received news of the D-Day Normandy landings and the fall of Rome with passing interest. Both Normandy and Rome were a very long way away.

The adaptable Royal Marine can usually turn his hand to anything and becoming mule handlers proved to be no exception. Marines were drawn from all troops to undertake this specialist training. How pleased were they leading the animals on a 16 mile march? The mules were sent to Dwarband to be 'battle inoculated.' S Tp provided the battle noises, firing 3" mortars, Vickers machine-guns and detonating explosive charges. The British love of animals was tried and tested on other occasions.

The Commando was operating among the Assam tea plantations and one of the tea-planters Mr.K.O. ('KO' or Knockout) Smith at Moniarkhal proved to be a very good friend to the marines of A and B Tps, both during the unit's stay and long after the war was over. Imagine the men's surprise when they first came face to face with Mrs Smith's pet deer, Wendy. The marines who hailed from Britain's cities were mesmerised by the fully grown deer who thought itself a dog!

'Knockout' Smith defused a potentially ugly incident when two marines happened upon a seriously injured cow lying alongside the road. The animal was in its death throes and 'Royal' in his ignorance prepared to shoot the cow to put it out of its misery. The local native population who gathered around the unfortunate animal were less than impressed with the Sacred Cow being dispatched in such a manner. Mr Smith having heard the commotion arrived in time to explain the mysterious ways of the East to the two bootnecks. During the month, sport and social events were slotted in whenever possible. Football was the predominant sport played. However a new team game was about to be taken up with great enthusiasm. Netball! HQ Tp played the first trial game between themselves with a view to challenging C Tp at a later date.

Capt Watkins organised a combined A and B Tp concert party. Lt Col Horton saw the show and pronounced the event a great success. If football, rugby, netball and concerts were not to an individual's taste, he could read one of the books brought to the unit by the Rev Kirkland's travelling library.

Towards the end of June rumour had it that the unit would soon be on the move. To improve the communications between Commando HQ and the patrol bases at Maniarkhal and Dwarband, new sites were sought in positions nearer to Silkuri. The proposed repositioning of the patrol bases would be subject to the weather conditions and transport available (one jeep, two mule carts and local sampans).

July 1944

The heavy rains continued to hamper the movement of the rifle troops back to new positions closer to Commando HQ. The unit received news that the Brigade would be relocating on or after 10th July. All 44's rifle troops were pulled back to either Silkuri or the area around Silchar railway station and placed on 48 hours' notice to move.

A small detachment (Lt Wintgens) made a 68 mile journey to Sylhet airfield to fly in Dakota transport aircraft dropping supplies (with and without parachutes) to troops in the field, east of Imphal. The detachment travelled in pairs, tasked with making their own travel arrangements to and from Sylhet. Every pair of men completed the trip successfully.

The Rev F.W.Cornwall RNVR joined the unit, immediately being taken out into the jungle country around the Aijal Track near Dwarband. Shortly afterwards he conducted the funeral of Mne D.Nelson (A Tp) at Silchar cemetery. The escort, firing party and pallbearers were provided by A Tp. This was the first fatality brought about by disease (cerebral malaria).

The wet weather continued to upset the sporting fixtures in the early days of July. Paradoxically, 11th July was recorded as the hottest day experienced since the unit arrived in the Far East. The date also signalled the start of the netball season. With the notable exception of A Tp, the unit became hooked. The way the games were contested held little comparison to those played in girls' schools. 44's marines never reached the standard of the Harlem Globetrotters but everyone enjoyed the game. The Commando staged two concert parties in Silchar cinema. A and B Tps performed in front of a packed house (including Brig. Nonweiler) and later in the month C, X and S Tps had similar success. With so much talent available, it naturally followed that individual 'troop artistes' should combine to form a unit concert party.

Although it was not recognized by the rank and file at the time, 24th July marked the date when Lt Col Horton became destined for higher things. The first step was when he was detached to take over command of 3 Special Service Brigade in the absence of Brig Nonweiler. 44 in company with 5 Commando moved out of Assam on 26th July to entrain for the long journey south to Bangalore in India. With the CO away, Capt Sturges was placed in command of the unit for the coming move.

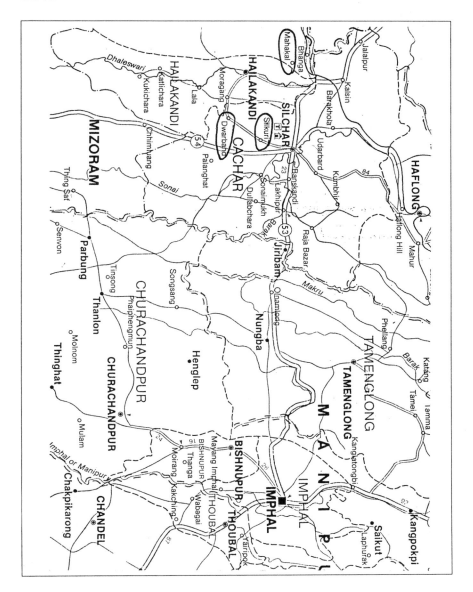

5
India and Ceylon

The Indian Railway System

From the time 44 landed in India until the end of hostilities, the Commando travelled over 2000 miles by rail. The journey south from Silchar to Bangalore was the most memorable.

The Indian railway system dates from the middle of the nineteenth century. The Marquis of Dalhousie (Governor General 1848-56) was actively involved in planning the initial rail network linking the major cities of the sub-continent. Lord Dalhousie strongly recommended a uniform gauge railway, stating when addressing the subject of track size: 'The gauge to be the one which science and experience may unite in selecting the best.' A high ideal, never attained.

In Europe locomotives ran on two divergent line gauges, the Broad Gauge (seven foot) and the narrower four foot-eight inch track. The latter size, used in Great Britain, had many supporters in India. It was a haphazard dimension, derived from the early days of railway building. A steam locomotive's primary function at the time was seen as a mechanism to pull coal carts along tracks laid within the confines of the collieries. Arguments continued over the gauge to be adopted: civil engineering problems, tunnels, bridges, cuttings, all swayed the principal protagonists' views. Lord Dalhousie suggested a compromise: a track gauge of five foot-six inch. This measurement would provide a greater advantage than the British gauge whilst maintaining most, if not all, of the best features of the seven foot gauge. The compromise was deemed acceptable to all interested parties and plans were laid to link the cities of Delhi, Allahabad, Calcutta, Madras, Calicut and Bombay using five foot-six inch 'Main Lines' run by six state owned companies. Lord Dalhousie's grand plan was duly implemented, only to be held up by the events leading to the Indian Mutiny in 1857. For 44's marines, the numerous train journeys would have been much smoother and more comfortable if all of India's railways had been built to one gauge.

By 1870 the network was expanding over the whole country. To a large extent the terrain dictated the route and urgent consideration was given to using the British gauge and/or one of two 'narrow' gauges (three foot-six inch or two foot-nine inch). Narrow gauge railways were being used successfully in other parts of the world. In India there was strong support for both sizes. The Governor General of the time (Lord

Mayo) followed his predecessor's example, suggesting a compromise gauge of three foot-three inch. With military bases, camps and outposts spread across India, railways were to play an important part in the transportation of men and equipment. The three foot-three inch (Metre Gauge) stemmed from considerations in respect of the size of wagons required to carry horses and gun-carriages. Once adopted, the metre gauge was used on all 'feeder' routes being built to link smaller towns to the broad gauge main line routes. The marine Commandos became very adept at transferring themselves and their equipment between trains of different gauges. At the time a play on Winston Churchill's famous words was popular; Never was so much baggage humped, so many times, by so few, in such a short time.

The northern hill areas still presented a problem for the railway engineers. The terrain around Darjeeling, Kalka and Simla decreed that an even smaller gauge would be required if rail links to the hill towns were to be introduced. Tracks measuring two foot-six inches and even two foot were constructed. 44 had already experienced the rigours of travelling on a narrow gauge line when the unit raced up to Silchar.

By 1900 it was being argued that India had not seen substantial benefits from using more than one gauge of line. A strong lobby of opinion suggested that as the metre gauge permanent way had been built wider than was necessary, it would be feasible to scrap both the existing gauges and provide more miles of double track by converting the whole system to the British four foot-eight inch gauge! The debate had come full circle in the space of fifty years.

Train journey Silchar to Bangalore
27th July-3rd August 1944

Reveille at Silkuri camp was sounded at 0500 hours. The Commando sat down to an early breakfast before moving off to Silchar railway station to join 5 and Brigade HQ for the long jaunt down through India. The Assam-Bengal Railway Company were surprisingly efficient, the train moving off on time at 1000 hours. This surprised the final party of men who arrived at the station with five minutes to spare.

Day One:

The narrow gauge railway stock was of very poor quality. The men were crowded together preventing any chance of being able to lie down during the night journey ahead. The Silchar branch line joined the

Talap-Chittagong line at Badarpur, a town accustomed to seeing military personnel pass through. In 1824 British troops met and defeated a raiding force during the Anglo-Burmese War (1824-26) near to the town. When the train halted in wooded countryside around Mymensingh (Assam) monkeys swarmed out of the trees to clamber over the locomotive and carriages. The Commandos, having little knowledge of the primates' habits, rapidly dived for cover when coming 'under fire' from any loose and available article hurled at them by the army of monkeys that had gathered around the train. After seeing action at Alethangyaw and Maungdaw, to be wounded by a piece of coal thrown from the coal-tender by a jabbering, long-armed, hairy little monster did not bear thinking about. The Commandos beat a hasty retreat back to the safety of the carriages and the train pulled away to continue the journey west across Assam towards Bengal.

Day Two:

The marines arrived at Jagnnathganj, a village situated on the western bank of the Brahmaputra River during the early afternoon. The two Commandos began the transfer of themselves and their equipment onto the steamship that was to take the Brigade across the river. The marines crowded onto the ship, only to discover that the vessel was not large enough to transport the complete unit on one trip. Two troops (B & X) were landed to await the vessel's return from its passage across the Brahmaputra River to Sirajganj, the largest town in North Bengal. On landing the Commandos transferred their stores and equipment from the ship onto the waiting train. All ranks were pleased to note that the Eastern Bengal railway line was broad gauge with carriages providing a reasonable level of comfort. Once the stores were loaded the Brigade settled down to wait for the ferry to return with the two troops left on the west bank of the river. An earthquake in 1897 changed the course of the Brahmaputra and the village was now three miles from the ferry dock thus ruling out any chance of sight-seeing.

Day Three:

The ferry returned from Jagnnathganj for the second time at 0300 hours: B and X Tps immediately entrained allowing the Brigade to continue its travels. Breakfast was eaten at 0930 hours when the train stopped at Ishurdi. Here the complete meal was prepared in the train's kitchen car by 44's cooks who catered for the entire Brigade. The route from now on took a course south towards the final destination. In the late afternoon the train halted at Chitpur, approximately four miles from India's second largest city Calcutta. All ranks took the opportunity to bathe and generally freshen up. With numerous military canteens in the immediate area all ranks went looking for 'big eats' before the night ride south continued.

Day Four:

During the day several halts were made for varying reasons: coal and water for the engine, priority rail traffic, crossing rail junctions, signal hold-ups. During these stoppages the soldiers and marines paraded for weapons and ammunition inspections and to eat. The line followed a route parallel to the coastline and when the train reached Khordha at 1900 hours it was running 13 hours behind schedule. Initiative is writ large in any Royal Marine officer's psyche and two of 44's subalterns decided to realize the dream of small boys everywhere and drive a steam train. The two young lieutenants invited the train driver to help the fireman while they took it in turns to drive the locomotive. The train careered down through India at a considerable rate of knots with a very worried driver extolling the virtues of caution and the dangers of over excess. By the end of the day the lost time had been made up, plus a few hours to spare!

Day Five:

At midday the train pulled into Waltair, a town close to the port of Vizagapatam. Sporting a station canteen befitting the junction where the trains of the Bengal/Nagpur and Madras Railway Companies meet, the Commandos were able to purchase a variety of goods including tinned fruit and milk. During the two hour break, the soldiers and marines carried out weapons inspections and the odd spot of physical training. The next stop was near Cocanada, a town situated at the top of a sea bay, the headquarters of the local district administration and the temporary home of 1 and 42(RM) Commandos. An unexpected welcome was received from 1's officers and 44's own rear party. The marines were the more popular as they brought with them a large delivery of mail. The letters from home were always a boost to morale. One or two bootnecks also received signed photographs of their favourite female film stars. To while away the time during Operation Screwdriver, some of A Tp's marines had written to Jean Kent, Barbara

Stanwyck, Margaret Lockwood and in a somewhat bizarre moment to Robert Young! 'Royal' shot a terrible line regarding jungle conditions, the heathen enemy, the heat, the wet, the bullets whizzing past their heads etc., etc. The very tall stories were worthy of an Errol Flynn movie.

Day Six:

The long, sometimes tedious journey continued throughout the day and night. During the midday break all weapons were inspected and fresh rations were taken on board. The route went away from the coast north of Madras, the train travelling south-west across the face of India.

Day Seven:

With 1000 rail miles under their belts the Brigade was unquestionably train hardened by the time the Commandos reached Trivellore in time to enjoy breakfast. Being the centre of the Vadegalai sect of the Hindu religion, the town boasted four temples. By now it was second nature for all ranks to inspect their personal weapons at each stop. After eating, the journey continued, the train now 12 hours behind schedule but the end of the journey was in sight.

Day Eight:

During the journey of approximately 1350 miles, the young men of the Brigade witnessed many aspects of Indian life. Beggers with horribly deformed limbs, char-wallahs always present whenever the train stopped, children jostling for money and sweets. The scenery was sometimes intensely boring, although on other occasions the natural beauty of the surroundings took the marines' breath away.

The Brigade arrived in Bangalore at 0530 hours. All ranks detrained, forming up to board motor transport to drive to Thondebhavi, 39 miles north of Bangalore. The baggage party, provided by D and S Troops followed the unit to the new location later in the day. The camp offered ample accommodation including two canteens and a cinema. Lt Col Horton rejoined 44 during the day, speaking to his marines in the evening. He told the men that after spending their first leave in India, the Commando could expect to move to Ceylon (Sri Lanka) in a few weeks time.

Bangalore
4th-29th August 1944

The marines quickly settled into their new camp, completing all unit and personal administration within the first few days. Once the managerial tasks were completed 75% of the Commando were granted 14 days' leave. Most of the men elected to spend their time in nearby Bangalore. The historic city was founded in 1537, slowly increasing in size until it became the administrative headquarters of Mysore State in 1831. Lt Carryer with a staff of nine set up an office to look after the interests and welfare of the men on leave in the city. Some members of the unit elected to travel onwards to other Indian cities, Madras, Bombay, Calcutta, Dacca to spend their leave. The marines discovered the cultural delights of India, enjoying the sights, sounds, entertainment, food and drink, not necessarily in that order. The local Army Commander, impressed by the general high standard of smartness, bearing and saluting of the marines, wrote a letter to the CO congratulating him on the personal discipline shown by his men. Lt Col Horton expected nothing less!

The remnants of the unit who remained in Thondebhavi Camp were busy preparing for the expected move to Ceylon (Sri-Lanka). Capt Sturges, Lt Owen and 29 other ranks provided the advance party, leaving the camp during the second week of August.

Capt H.G.S.Saunders transferred into the unit from 42(RM) Commando, being placed in command of D Tp. Two weeks later he was promoted to major. The officers' mess hosted a social gathering for the Brigade Commander and the commanding officers of other regiments stationed in the vicinity. Shortly after this function, Lt Col Horton and Maj Macafee (2i/c) lunched with Brig Nonweiler: things were afoot!

The orders for the move to Ceylon were received, the unit would move between 30th August and 2nd September.

The bulk of the men returned from leave on 22nd August. On the following day the internal structure of the Commando was altered with the formation of 'Y' Troop. Commanded by Lt Rider, the new troop would include all the Commando's clerks, drivers, cooks, armourers and so on. With the move to Ceylon imminent, the marines were sharpened up following their leave. The remaining days commenced with full Commando parades/Naval Divisions followed by strenuous physical training sessions.

Before leaving, 44 received a visit from Lt Col Riches (GSO 1 Special Service Group) who lectured selected personnel on 1 & 4 Special Service Brigades' accomplishments during the Normandy landings.

Train journey: Bangalore to Trincomalee
30th August-2nd September 1944.

The marines of 44 were to see more of the Indian sub-continent from the train carriage window. To herald the start of the third lengthy railway journey, reveille was sounded at 0545 hours. The unit arrived at Bangalore's Cantonment Station at 0830 hours, loading stores and equipment before leaving at 1105 hours. The train stopped at Jalarpet Junction in the early evening; the carriages were comfortable, allowing most men to have a good night's rest.

Arriving at Karur at 0700 hours on 31st August the marines ate breakfast prior to the train reaching its destination, Trichinopoly. The Commando unloaded its kit, stores and equipment before transferring to the metre gauge railway which was to take them down to the ferry dock. For the onward journey 44 was divided between two trains. C and D Tps plus the stores left at 2000 hours followed by the remainder of the unit at 2115 hours.

After travelling through the night the two trains arrived at Dhanushkodi at 0445 and 0715 hours on 1st September respectively. The loading of men, stores and equipment onto the ferry commenced in the afternoon, being completed 15 minutes before the ship cast off at 2300 hours.

The journey from India to Ceylon (Sri Lanka) across the 22 mile Pulk Strait lasted two hours. The train to take 44 to Trincomalee was scheduled to leave at 0700 hours on 2nd September. After leaving the ferry in the early hours, the marines spent the night on a nearby beach.

The Ceylonese train accommodation was exceptionally bereft of any creature comforts. The marines' excellent discipline, patience and good humour enabled them to see through a day of discomfort and intense boredom.

After stopping at Maho, 'Royal' was thankful when the train finally arrived at Trincomalee at 1845 hours. Transport and a good hot meal put all ranks in a better frame of mind.

Trincomalee
3rd September-14th October 1944

The island of Ceylon (Sri Lanka) possesses beautiful scenery and lush vegetation, tall ferns, rhododendrons, palms, with large forests of ebony and satinwood trees. Mine workings extracted minerals, the most important of which was graphite. Ceylon also boasted two ports. Columbo to the west, historically an important oiling station for vessels sailing to the Far East and Trincomalee, the natural deep water harbour on the east coast. The Headquarters of the Allied South East Asia Command was located in the centre of the island at Kandy, the old capital city. The significance of Ceylon was clear to see, with the protection against threat of invasion and air raids being of paramount importance (Columbo and Trincomalee had both been bombed earlier in 1944). 44 was promptly designated the immediate action Commando. The unit would provide one rifle troop, one section each of Vickers machine guns and 3" mortars on 30 minutes notice. The remainder of the Commando were on one hour standby.

44's officers: Trincomalee, Sept.-Oct. 1944

Front row: Capt C.A.Watkins; Capt K.P.Parish; Major G.H.Stockley; Lt Col F.C.Horton; Major H.G.S.Saunders; Capt E.M.Sturges; Capt S.C.Hellis. Middle row: Capt J.W.F.Richardson RAMC; Capt A.Martin; Lt S.C.Wintgens; Capt O.N.StJ.Hamlin; Lts J.I.H.Owen; P.H.Rider; W.W.H.Brydon; R.C.Steele; J.K.Lee; Rev R.Clarke. Back row: Lts D.H.Lewis; S.Henshall; A.E.Barrett; P.Shefford; A.R.White; C.N.C.Carryer; R.G.Acton; G.P.A.Bleasdell. Absent: Capt Macan.

The marines' stay in 'Trinco' was dominated by training exercises, internal security, a wedding and football! The first full day on camp was spent settling into the new quarters and unloading the baggage train. Unbeknown to the marines at the time, they were joined by one of their future commanding officers. On 8th September Major G.H.Stockley RM was posted to 44 as the second-in-command, replacing one of the original 3 RM officers Major J.L.A.Macafee (transferred to 3 Special Service Brigade Headquarters along with Lt G.D.Stewart). At the end of September Capt S.C.Hellis RM joined 44 to replace the recently departed Capt Coole as Admin Officer.

After their stint of internal security duties was completed the marines began training. Lt Col Horton approved the assault course and all ranks used the 30 yard range for zeroing (sight setting) all weapons.

The first troop exercise once again highlighted the dangers associated with using live ammunition to simulate the real thing. D Tp, out in the Royal Naval field firing area, were practising section attacks when a 2" mortar bomb fell short, wounding a marine together with Lt White. This officer was removed to hospital where, due to the nature of the injury, an operation was necessary to remove a damaged eye. This unfortunate incident was followed one week later by a fatal training accident. 44's marines were spectators as 5 Tp, 1 Commando carried out an exercise assault against a defended beach using live ammunition. During the landing one man was hit and later died of his wounds. The utterly realistic training regime undertaken by Commando units, started at Achnacarry, had claimed yet another life.

On 28th September, 200 men from 44 took part in Exercise Turtle. The Commandos provided the enemy, set against 600 Royal Marines drawn from ships of the Eastern Fleet. The Fleet marines were to land from the sea to attack a fictional radar station sited three miles inland from the beach. 44's task was to oppose the landing force, using Japanese tactics learned so well at Alethangyaw. The allotted task was to harass the raiders both as they approached and withdrew from their objective. The Commandos marched out of camp during the evening preceding the dawn raid, sleeping in the jungle after preparing their defences. The Fleet marines landed in two waves at 0600 and 0620 hours, the first wave getting extremely wet in the process. Although the raiders tired very quickly during the push through the thick jungle, the target was captured by 1000 hours. During the withdrawal back to the beach, 44's jungle marines mounted continuous attacks, usually from the rear. Small parties of Fleet marines were effortlessly isolated in the jungle surroundings to be captured or 'killed' by their enemy. Among other things, the Fleet marines learned that a man was required to be very fit to survive in the jungle. 44's 'enemy' detachment had put into practice most of their recently gained jungle expertise, doing so without the benefit of direction from the junior NCOs; all the corporals and lance corporals were on a refresher course!

Unit training reached a peak during the period 1st-7th October. All troops carried out the Beach Assault Demolition exercise demonstrated by 1 previously, thankfully without incurring any casualties. Troop exercised against troop, practising movement and control in close country. One exercise involved elements of B Tp landing on the beach from Catalina flying boats as a prelude to attacking the nearby Naval Air Station. Officers, in addition to the troop exercises, went pistol shooting, practised map and compass work and went swimming; wearing full fighting order! The CO was always to be seen either inspecting individual troops before they went into the jungle or presenting himself to the marines in the most unexpected locations.

'Trinco' provided a safe anchorage for many capital ships of the Royal Navy and small groups of 44's marines made goodwill visits to the ships anchored in the harbour, including HM Ships *Queen Elizabeth*, *Renown* and *Adamant*. At regular intervals, the Royal Marine bands from the ships came ashore to entertain the unit. The officers' mess hosted a mess night for the Brigade's officers and the COs of the three Commandos. The officers mess also received a visit from the new Deputy Brigade Commander, Colonel P.Young DSO, MC, following his recent arrival from the UK.

European men, soldiering in the Far East had from time immemorial been struck down by tropical disease. In 1943 the ratio of illness to wounded in the 14th Army was an incredible 120:1. Dysentery, malaria and other fevers, jungle sores, mite typhus all accounted for thousands of cases requiring evacuation from forward areas. Of these, the largest single health problem was malaria, accounting for over 75% of all sickness. The word malaria was derived from two Italian words meaning 'bad air' as people associated the condition with the musty foul smelling air of the swamp regions. The disease, carried by parasites living partly in man's red blood cells and partly in the female 'Anopheles' mosquitoe fly, is spread by the insect when it bites.

Malaria produces acute attacks of chills, fever, sweats and general debility. One strain (vivax or tertian) produces recurrent bouts of fever. Until the Second World War the disease was usually treated with quinine, however when supplies from the East Indies were cut, new compounds were hurriedly developed. Mepacrine, Atabrine, Chloroquine and Primaquine all proved to be effective in fighting the disease. By the time that 3 Special Service Brigade arrived in India the position had been considerably improved. Malaria Forward Treatment Units, set up in locations within 24 hours travel time of the battle zones ensured that malaria cases were treated far more quickly; men returning to the front in around three weeks. This compared favourably with the months a man was previously away from his unit when cases were usually transported back to base hospitals in India. The 54 India General Hospital in Ceylon invariably treated 44's cases of malaria. In the first week of October, 100 marines of all ranks were hospitalized. Although sickness reached its peak during this period, illnesses of various types were always present to deplete the ranks of the Commando in common with all other units of the Brigade.

If the marines were not watching or playing sport they could visit the No. 17 Mobile Cinema Unit to see a batch of Ministry of Information films including The Nazi Strikes, Divide and Conquer, Battle of Britain and The Battle for Rome. In a lighter vein the cinema unit also screened a film entitled You Were Never Lovelier.

On 8th October Lt Col Grant RM (SEAC Staff) brought the orders for the expected move. The Commando was to leave on 15th October for an undisclosed destination. For the Staff Officer's benefit, S Tp demonstrated their expertise using both 2" and 3" mortars and Vickers machine guns in close support of a rifle troop. The marines knew that an operation was in the wind when the unit was ordered to 'paint or dye' all white clothing and equipment.

The enjoyable stay in 'Trinco' was rounded off in fine style with a wedding! One of 44's officers from 3RM days, Lt Rider married 3rd Officer Pamela Edgeworth, WRNS whom he had met on board the *Reina del Pacifico* during the ship's voyage out to India. The ceremony was conducted in St Stephen's Church and turned out to be a 44 day to remember. Capt Sturges was the best man and Lt Col Horton, gave away the bride. The newly married couple were borne away from the church in a jeep, pushed by a group of 44's officers. Forty years later when the couple celebrated their wedding anniversary, they invited as many of the original guests as could be found. When the party departed from the function suite they were surprised to see a World War Two jeep waiting at the kerbside. Although the couple climbed aboard and the same group of officers (of an age) agreed to recreate the 'Trinco' push, most insisted on some assistance from the vehicle's engine!

Train journey Trincomalee-Madras
15th-18th October 1944

Train journeys were eternally linked to early reveilles (0500 hours). At 0800 hours, 15th October, the Commandos paraded in marching order plus bed rolls before boarding buses for the journey to Trincomalee station. The return trip back to the ferry point was a re-run of the outward journey. A meal was taken when the train stopped at Maho before the journey continued on throughout the night. The carriages were cramped and uncomfortable, preventing most men from getting any sleep. The marines were relieved when they finally arrived at Talaimannar pier at 0630 hours, 16th October. The transfer between train and ship went on throughout the morning. The ferry cast off in the early afternoon and the Commando disembarked back on the

Indian mainland at Danushkodi at 1600 hours. Fitness training was provided in the form of transferring stores and equipment from ferry to train.

More overnight rail travel began when the train pulled out at 2300 hours. The 17th October was spent travelling north through the state of Madras towards the major rail junction at Trichinopoly, still 250 miles from Madras city. On arrival the train stopped for two hours and the local Auxiliary Womens Voluntary Service (AWVS) dispensed free food and cigarettes. The final leg of the journey to the port of Madras began when the train departed in the early evening. After an uneventful journey through the night the Commandos arrived in Madras at 0700 hours, 18th October. Another group of AWVS ladies were on hand to give out tea and cigarettes again before 44 embarked on SS *Rajula* in company with their usual travelling companions, 5 Commando and Brigade HQ.

Sea Time III
Madras to Chittagong
19th-23rd October 1944

The *Rajula* (British India Steam Navigation Co) had been actively involved with the services since 1941 when she assisted in the evacuation of Singapore. The vessel went on to take part in the Sicily Landings in 1943. When 44 became acquainted with the ship, she was being used as an ambulance transport vessel, conveying the wounded from Burma back to Indian ports. On her return trip the vessel carried fresh troops to the war zone.

Built on the Clyde in 1926 the vessel had been designed especially for service in the Far East, often being used to transport Islamic pilgrims to Jeddah, the nearest port to the holy shrine at Mecca. The *Rajula* was driven by twin screws, the two triple expansion steam engines giving a service speed of 15 knots. Unbeknown to the marines, the *Rajula* was the sister ship of the ill-fated *Rohna*, hit and sunk by a German glider bomb in the Mediterranean.

The *Rajula* was to live in the memory of 44's marines as the ship responsible for the unit acquiring the nickname 'Horton's Pirates.' The food served to the 'troops on board was little more than swill, being almost inedible. The catering arrangements became so abysmal that Lt Col Horton was prompted to enter into a 'frank and meaningful' dialogue with the ship's master. Every officer and marine supported the Colonel wholeheartedly. The report of the heated exchange of views between Colonel and Captain becoming legend throughout the

Commando. No-one could ever remember seeing the CO so nettled.

The short sea voyage across the Bay of Bengal was used, as always, for training. The usual ship's routine took over: lifeboat drills, air raid alerts and darken-ship exercises were all practised.

The upper deck space allocated for training was extremely limited. In addition to daily physical training, all troops carried out weapons training: the 2" mortar teams firing their weapons over the side. The ever popular tug of war was the only competitive physical sport that the two Commandos could set up in the space available. A knockout competition was rapidly organised, teams being entered by all troops from both units, plus teams from Brigade HQ. Successful against strong teams in the earlier rounds, the final was pulled between 44's A Tp and 3 Tp, 5 Commando; the Army Commandos won.

The ship arrived in Chittagong, the chief port of Eastern Bengal at 1300 hours, 22nd October. The marines remained on board until the following day. The Commando subsequently transferred onto five LCI's[9] to sail in convoy, leaving Chittagong during the early evening, 23rd October. Some, but not all the landing craft provided a cold meal from reserve rations: not all captains were that thoughtful. The flotilla sailed around the southern tip of St Martin's Island during the night, passing Alethangyaw, 44's first operational area, before proceeding up the Naf River to Teknaf.

Teknaf
24th October 1944-2nd January 1945

After disembarking from the LCIs 44 formed up to march to the Brigade's lines to join the other three Commandos in a very cramped makeshift camp. Until such times as the Brigade received a supply of tents, all units constructed their own living quarters and ingenuity would know no bounds. Using bamboo poles and jungle vegetation 'Royal' went about erecting the basic shelters known throughout Burma as 'bashas.'

On 25th October, as the men put together their jungle huts, little did they realise that Lt Col Horton was about to leave the unit. When the

---

9   Landing Craft Infantry (Large). Constructed of steel, length 158', beam 23', draught
      4'10". Twin screws powered by eight diesel engines (four to each propeller) gave a
      service speed of 12 knots. Capable of carrying 205 troops plus 32 tons of stores on
      sea voyages with a crew of four officers and 24 ratings. Armament five 20mm
      cannon.

Commando paraded at 1730 hours the marines fully expected to be told of some future operation. However the Colonel, to everyone's complete surprise, broke the news of his imminent departure, going on to wish all ranks 'Goodbye, good luck and a safe, early journey home.' The whole parade was aghast, numerous men spontaneously shouted out 'Why?' and most of the assembled marines sat down on the parade ground in a show of unrehearsed unity. The Colonel had been the unit's Commanding Officer since the closing days of 3rd Battalion, Royal Marines. He had completed the Achnacarry course alongside his marines, led the Commando with exceptionally fine judgement and flair during the fighting at Alethangyaw and had always been a fair and gentlemanly Royal Marine officer. The personal loyalty he evoked in every man under his command was unique. 44 was very unhappy!

When Lt Col Horton left the following morning he was given a rousing send off by his officers and marines. Major G.H.Stockley, who had assumed command travelled with the outgoing commanding officer to Brigade Headquarters. A feeling of acute unease ran through the unit as the marines cleaned their lines in readiness for an inspection by the Deputy Brigade Commander. There is little record of the Brigade Commander's reaction to 44's protests. When Maj Stockley returned to the unit later in the day, he brought with him the news that Lt Col Horton was likely to rejoin the unit in the near future. (He returned to 44 on 30th October.)

During Lt Col Horton's absence the marines continued to clean the camp, pitch tents, build galleys, dig defence trenches and seek out suitable training areas. Brig Nonweiler inspected 44's efforts during the intervening period, no doubt gauging the mood of the men at the same time. With the CO's reappearance the morale of the unit soared. The day following the Colonel's return, he accompanied the Deputy Brigade Commander to watch D Tp exercising with a mortar section in close support; needless to say the training was carried out using live ammunition.

November 1944

During the first week of the month 3 Special Service Brigade was visited by Lieutenant General Sir A.F.P.Christison KBE, CB, MC, (GOC XV Indian Corps). The General watched a Brigade training display; 44's contribution was carried out by A Tp (Capt Watkins). The marines demonstrated the finer points of Japanese cunning, tactics and favoured booby traps. This realistic display claimed a casualty when a marine was shot through the hand, the wound was serious enough to warrant his immediate removal to Nhila hospital. Later in the week Brig

J.A.Hirst DSO, commander, 74 Infantry Brigade, 25 Indian Infantry Division, paid the Commandos a visit. It was likely that some of them would come under his command when elements of the Special Service Brigade returned to the fighting in the Arakan region.

Training continued, including Troop exercises using Goatley[10] boats. On one of the night exercises A Tp formed a box so successfully that they remained undiscovered in the face of concerted efforts by the Adjutant and other HQ Tp officers to find them.

The marines mastered the doubtful art of firing hand-held 2" mortars. When addressed with competence and confidence, firing the small mortar 'from the hip' could be carried out successfully: B Tp proved the point. B Tp also put their commando skills to good use to construct a 'toggle bridge' to replace the dilapidated timber structure that was being used to cross a nearby chaung. Time was also taken to set up an inter-troop tug of war competition.

Five officers plus 47 NCOs and marines joined 44 for a short period from HMS *Braganza*, the Naval Shore Establishment in Bombay. Whilst attached to the Commando the detachment was known as Z Tp.

The middle two weeks of November were dominated by operational plans and movements. 1 and 42 Commandos took up positions held by 74 Indian Infantry Brigade at West Chiradan, near Maungdaw. Two 3" mortar teams (Capt Steele) from 44 were attached to 1 for the operation and a sub-section of C Tp was detached to 42 to augment their Commando HQ defence platoon. The two Royal Marine Commandos were scheduled to change over later in the month (21st November). However the relief was postponed, albeit the remainder of C Tp did join 42 for a time during the operation.

For 5 and 44, waiting to relieve the two Commandos already in the field, the pace of events at Teknaf suddenly quickened. Both units were placed on immediate standby to participate in an independent action planned for the near future. A composite force was to be formed consisting of one battalion Yorks and Lancs Regiment, two rifle troops of 5 Commando, A and B Tps plus two armed stretcher units from X Tp, 44 (RM) Commando.

The combined force was to be commanded by Major Robin Stuart (2i/c of 5 Commando) and be known as Robforce. With all preparations made, the marines and soldiers keyed up, adrenalin flowing; the

---

10   A collapsible boat with canvas sides, wooden bottom and weighing 2-cwt. Capable of carrying seven men (six using paddles), two trained men could assemble the craft in one minute. These craft were not particularly seaworthy, but perfectly adequate on calm waters.

undisclosed operation was suddenly cancelled and the force disbanded.

Instead, the two Commandos, (5 and 44) 'waged war' against each other on 'Exercise Sarong.' 5 failed to penetrate 44's HQ box during the dark hours, which was the object of the exercise. Yet again the realistic training claimed a casualty: Lt P.Shefford receiving severe burns from an exploding 77 phosphorous grenade. He was removed to hospital for immediate surgery.

The planned interchange between the two Royal Marine Commandos having been cancelled, C Tp, (minus one sub-section) returned to the unit after being attached to 42 for one week. 1 Commando operating in tandem with 42 laid a well concealed ambush at Hinthaya, an area well known to 44 from the 'Operation Screwdriver' action. The Army Commandos killed 14 of the enemy and also managed to capture a Japanese soldier, the first prisoner to be taken by 25 Indian Infantry Division.

For 5 and 44 jungle training continued. Night attacks, signal exercises, troop v troop raids, all not without incident. One marine (B Tp) received a flesh wound in the lower buttock! As a break from jungle training, A Tp were busy practising their close order drill. They had been detailed to provide 44's contribution to the Brigade's Guard of Honour for the expected visit by Major General R.E.Laycock CB, DSO (Chief of Combined Operations). When A Tp had attained the precision and smartness associated with a 'King's Squad' passing out parade, the visit was postponed!

At Teknaf most of the men suffered recurring bouts of malaria. At any given time at least 50 men were hospitalised suffering from the effects of the disease as well as other fevers. To add to their woes Lt Col Horton left the Commando for the second time. The CO had been 'seconded to carry out detached duties of a permanent nature.' The marines of 44, realising that the military mind worked in mysterious ways were in a more philosophical mood when the Colonel finally departed. Major Stockley was promoted to lieutenant colonel and given command. However, to the average stoical bootneck, the whirlwind which hit the camp shortly after Lt Col Horton's departure spoke volumes!

December 1944

At the start of the month the Brigade was reunited with the return of 1 and 42 from Maungdaw. The first week of the month was filled with official visits, reorganisation and transfers. When the Deputy Brigade Commander, Col P.Young, paid 44 a visit it became clear that something was in the air. On the 4th December the Brigade was inspected by two generals: Maj Gen R.E.Laycock, DSO and Maj Gen A.R.Chater CB, DSO, RM (Director, Combined Operations, Far East). All four units allocated one troop to the combined Guard of Honour, X Tp coming from 44. 42's admirable pipe band provided the music. Following the parade Gen Laycock addressed each Commando individually.

December saw a general reorganisation of Britain's Commando Forces resulting in every Commando unit losing one rifle troop, a reduction from five troops to four. The shake-up divined that 44's D Tp was disbanded. The displaced personnel were sent to the other troops in the unit bringing them up to near full strength. The contentious title 'Special Service' Brigade was replaced by 'Commando' Brigade. Coinciding with these organisational changes Brig W.L.Nonweiler, who had led the Brigade since its inception in 1943 was relieved by Brigadier C.R.Hardy, DSO,* RM. Brig Hardy had led 46 (RM) Commando with distinction during the Normandy landings, being awarded two Distinguished Service Orders in the process. After leaving the Far East, Brig Nonweiler was sent to Northern Europe to assume command of 117 Infantry Brigade, Royal Marines. To complete the catalogue of changes 3 Commando Brigade was placed under the command of 26 Indian Infantry Division. Lastly 44 Commando lost two more of the original officers from 3RM days: Capt R.C.Steele and Lt S.C.Wintgens were moved to other positions within the Corps. At the same time 12 marines, all volunteers, joined 44 after serving on Royal Naval Air Stations.

The weeks leading up to Christmas were dominated by one single event: a visit to the Brigade by Lord Louis Mountbatten, accompanied by his Chief of Staff Lt Gen F.A.Browning DSO and Brig Hardy. Lord Louis duly arrived on 19th December to spend time with the Brigade. Twelve marines from 44 were temporarily transferred to the personal bodyguard assigned to protect the Supreme Commander during his overnight stay. Officers who had not previously met Lord Louis were introduced to him at Brigade HQ. As an intended tribute to Lord Louis, a guard of honour (Lt Owen) was paraded by 44 consisting of 18 NCOs and marines all of whom were over six feet tall. Unfortunately the unit's well meaning intentions were not well received by the Supreme Commander's staff; Lord Louis looked small in stature as he inspected the guard. Subsequently, no official photographs of the occasion were made available!

The Commando Brigade went on parade at 0730 hours on the morning following the Supreme Allied Commanders arrival. After walking through the ranks drawn up for his inspection, Lord Louis had the Commandos 'gather round' to hear his usual morale boosting address. Remembering Admiral Mountbatten's last visit to the Brigade prior to Operation Screwdriver, the soldiers and marines were in no doubt that an important operation was in the offing.

A series of three day Troop exercises, field firing exercises and pill box assaults was rounded off with a full scale amphibious night practice landing. Since the action at Alethangyaw, every opportunity had been taken to test all aspects of the unit's organisation and the night landing exercise was deemed a success. Both attacking formations (Hamforce and Macforce) accomplishing their allotted tasks of locating and attacking their respective targets. Between the training programmes a blitz was made to improve the camp's sanitary conditions; this action was also deemed a success.

Capt Watkins' theatrical accomplishments reached new heights when the Brigade Concert Party staged three separate performances of their Christmas show before enthusiastic audiences.

Two days before Christmas the Brigade received a visit from Maj Gen G.E.Lomax CB, CBE, DSO, MC (GOC 26 Indian Infantry Division). The yuletide festivities included the usual church services, a short gymkhana, the officers v SNCOs football match (5-1 to the SNCOs) and an excellent dinner; for some the best meal ever eaten since joining the Royal Marines. To round off the day 42's dance band played in the canteen.

Military activities were resumed on Boxing Day when Lt Gen Sir Philip Christison arrived to hold conferences with the Brigade Commander and his commanding officers. On 30th December the Brigade was put on 48 hours notice to move.

Amid the usual scenes of kit being packed, weapon inspections, stores and equipment being loaded, 44 managed to fit in the last of their inter-Commando football matches. The marines decisively beat the soldiers of their 'buddy' Commando 5 (4-0), but not before the goalkeeper, Mne Norman (S Tp) managed to break two of his fingers.

On New Year's Eve the CO attended conferences throughout the day at Brigade HQ. On his return troop leaders conferences were held well into the late evening and there were certainly no celebrations held to herald in the New Year 1945. On New Year's morning, Lt Col Stockley addressed the Commando, outlining 44's involvement in the forthcoming operations. At 1230 hours the marines were gathered together again to hear Brig Hardy speculate on what lay ahead for the Commando Brigade.

44 moved out during the forenoon 2nd January, embarking onto two LCIs: A, B, C and HQ Tps in the first with Rear HQ, S and X Tps following. The embarkation was recorded for posterity by several official war photographers. The mess decks on both vessels became crowded with marines and their equipment. Some men resorted to sleeping on deck when the convoy anchored in the River Naf for the

night in company with HM Destroyers *Napier* and *Nepal*. At first light
all the assembled ships moving off, sailing south towards Akyab Island.

6
Return to the Arakan

Operation Talon (Akyab)
3rd-11th January 1945

The Allied offensive to drive south down through the Arakan started on 12th December and by January 1945 the advance was well under way. Lt Gen Christison, well aware of the Commando's amphibious capabilities, proposed using the Brigade to outflank the retreating Japanese 28th Army in a series of landings, given the codename 'Talon.' The first task would be to land on Akyab, a low lying island covering an area of approximately five square miles and situated at the mouth of the Kaladan River. The surrounding area consisted of paddy fields interspersed by a few wooded areas. With the exception of two small hills (25-30 feet) the island was flat but intersected by numerous chaungs, creeks and mangrove swamps: the beach provided an easy landing area. In the early days of the twentieth century the region had the reputation of being a 'white man's grave.' Effectively the chief port of the Arakan district the Akyab waterfront provided ample dock facilities. Once occupied, the iron wharfs, a stone pier, timber jetties and the deep water anchorage outside the harbour would be used to create a first class and essential supply base for the land forces pushing south. In addition to the docks and harbour the island also possessed an airstrip. The Japanese had flown from Akyab when mounting air attacks on the docks in Calcutta and Chittagong. By capturing the airfield intact, the Allied air defence of the island and air cover for the advancing troops would be guaranteed.

The Commando Brigade was to spearhead a full scale assault by 26th Indian Infantry Division on Akyab. The RAF and USAAF would provide air cover with no less than 21 squadrons of P47 Thunderbolts, P38 Lightnings, B25 Mitchell bombers, Hurribombers, Spitfires, Beauforts and Hurricanes.

Naval gunfire support would be provided by HM Cruisers *Newcastle*, *Nigeria* and *Phoebe* together with the Destroyers *Pathfinder*, *Rapid* and *Roebuck*. The landing craft transporting the Commandos would steer a seven mile course to the shoreline before depositing the Brigade at a point north-east of the British Overseas Airway Corporation's jetty.

At the planning stage of the operation intelligence reports indicated that three battalions of enemy troops occupied the island. Beach defences included fortified bunkers, anti-tank ditches and barbed wire between the high and low water marks.

The convoy carrying the Commando Brigade weighed anchor and set off at 0400 hours, 3rd January, sailing down the Arakan coast to carry out the major assault against fortified beach defences. The Commandos, keyed up and ready for the expected opposed landing, had no way of knowing that the Japanese had left Akyab two days earlier. A Royal Artillery officer, flying over the island on the previous day noted that the villagers were waving enthusiastically at his light aircraft. Seeing this the aeroplane landed to be greeted by friendly natives who confirmed that no enemy troops remained on the island. A tremendous feeling of anti-climax swept over the Brigade. The Corps Commander made the decision to land as intended, the first wave of LCAs[11] setting off in tidy lines at 1015 hours. From their LCIs the marines watched the three cruisers and attendant destroyers move to their support positions as planned. 44, designated Brigade Reserve, landed in the early afternoon.

44 going to war: Teknaf, January 1945

---

11   Landing Craft Assault: Wooden construction with ramped bow door. Length 41'6" x Beam 10' x Draught 2' 3" (ideal for the shallow chaungs). Load: 35 troops plus 800lb of equipment. Twin Ford V8 engines driving a single propeller produced a speed of seven knots. Twin rudders. Crew: four. Armament: one twin Lewis gun, one Bren gun.

Shortly after landing 44 moved off the beach to protect the road used by motor transport and tanks of the 19th Indian Lancers. The unit boxed for the night around Donbyin village. During the early hours elements of 74 Brigade passed through the marines lines to continue the advance.

4th January:

By early morning 74 Brigade had completed its transit through the Commando's positions. The marines then carried out a general inspection of the immediate area, discovering a derelict enemy company HQ position guarded by two dummy armoured fighting vehicles; the 'tanks' constructed of bamboo and other jungle vegetation. The graves of two Japanese soldiers and a quantity of useless material was also found. During the afternoon, Rear HQ, X and S Tps rejoined the Commando after spending the previous night on local defence duties elsewhere. The CO received orders for 44 to prepare to land and occupy the adjacent Baronga Islands which lay to the south-east of Akyab. The night passed peacefully and the marines took the opportunity to buy chickens from the local population to enhance the contents of the standard ration packs. As these rations included dehydrated goat, the scrawny chickens on offer were a popular substitute.

5th January:

Shortly after midday the Commando marched to Fakir Point in preparation for the passage out to the 'Barongas.' The marines were 'billeted' in the residential area of the small town and applied themselves to constructing bashas of several very individual designs. During the day the brigade commander landed on the main Baronga island following reports that the enemy had left: subsequently 44's role was changed to patrolling the islands using LCAs based near the unit's location at the 'Point.'

6th January:

With Fakir Point (popular for swimming) designated 44's base area, camp facilities were speedily reorganised with the temporary bashas being upgraded to provide a more permanent and comfortable home.

The whole area took on the aura of a shanty town. A marine of A Tp was accidentally shot and killed as his section prepared to carry out a patrol to the Baronga islands. At the same time B Tp sent out a patrol to Savage Island, neither patrol reported any sign of enemy activity.

7th January:

In addition to patrolling the three Barongas and Savage Island, parties from X Tp went out to Walken and No Name islands. On both islands the local population appeared friendly, although obviously very scared of retribution should the Japanese return.

8th January:

At 0200 hours Lt Col Stockley assembled the Troop Leaders to inform them that the Brigade was to make an opposed landing at Myebon within the next few days. The day was spent preparing equipment, swimming, exploring old Japanese defences around Fakir Point and looking at the ruined town.

9th/10th January:

The marines waited in anticipation for the order to move out. However, the operation was postponed for 24 hours due to adverse weather conditions. During the afternoon of the 9th 44 had a grandstand view of an enemy air attack on the shipping anchored offshore. Five of the eight attacking aeroplanes were shot down by RAF Spitfires already established on Akyab's airfield. News that the Brigade would definitely land at Myebon on the 12th January prompted a last minute flurry of activity. as part of the normal routine, troop leaders and NCOs studied air photographs and maps of the area and all the relevant information was passed down to the marines.

11th January:

At midday the Commando formed up to march back to their original landing beach to board LCMs[12] for transfer out to minesweepers anchored in the harbour roads. Although the accommodation was limited, the crews of the 'sweepers' made their passengers as comfortable as possible and provided the all important cup of hot sweet tea throughout the remainder of the day and the following morning.

Operation Passport (Myebon)
12th-21st January 1945

The Myebon Peninsula lays 30 miles to the south east of Akyab Island, projecting from the Burmese mainland into Hunters Bay. Less that a mile wide with several hilly features, the peninsula is set between the estuaries of the Kyatsin River (west) and the Myebon River (east). Large tracts of the area are covered in dense jungle and bamboo.

The capture of Myebon was essential to Lt Gen Christison's overall strategy for two main reasons:

a) control of the two main waterways (Kyatsin River and Daignbon Chaung) would deny a waterborne escape route to enemy forces;

b) the area would provide a firm base from which to operate during the proposed attack on Kangaw.

Tactical considerations ruled out the possibility of the Brigade being put ashore from any of the inland chaungs to the north due to:

1) a long approach depriving the attacking force of any element of surprise.

2) a convoy of landing craft travelling in single line ahead would present a prime target for enemy ambush.

3) the narrow waterways being blocked by either a broken down craft or by obstructions placed by the enemy.

4) the dense jungle running down to the river banks prohibiting the provision of effective air cover.

Taking the above points into account, the staff planning officers

---

12   Landing Craft (Mechanised), Mark 1: steel construction with ramped bow door. Length 44'8" x beam 14' x draught 2'6". Capable of carrying various load combinations: Tank or truck (maximum 16 tons), or one 25-pdr gun and DUKW, or two x 37mm anti-tank guns and two weapons carriers or six Jeeps. These craft were powered by two 60hp Chrysler engines, each driving a single propeller producing a speed seven knots. Crew: six. Armament: two Lewis guns.

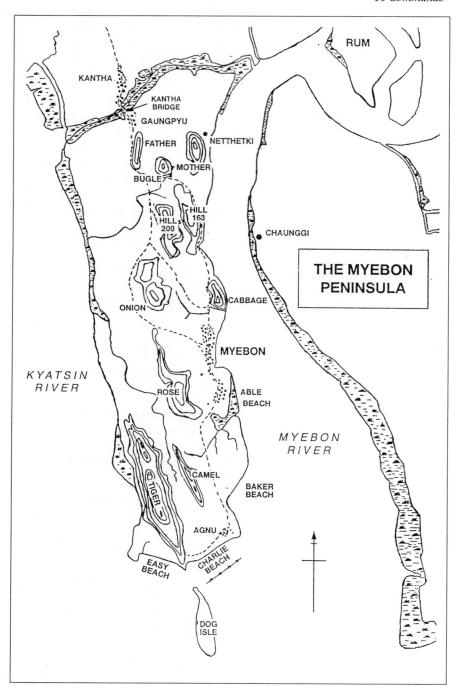

RUM

KANTHA

KANTHA
BRIDGE

GAUNGPYU

FATHER   NETTHETKI

MOTHER

BUGLE

HILL
163

HILL
200

CHAUNGGI

**THE MYEBON
PENINSULA**

ONION

CABBAGE

MYEBON

*KYATSIN
RIVER*

ROSE   ABLE
BEACH

*MYEBON
RIVER*

CAMEL

TIGER

BAKER
BEACH

AGNU

EASY
BEACH

CHARLIE
BEACH

DOG
ISLE

made the decision that an assault should be made from the sea at a point near to the southern tip of the peninsula. The most suitable beaches were situated near the village of Agnu. The shoreline was covered by black sand with a combination of surface silt and thick mud at low tide. Intelligence reports indicated that Myebon was defended by six infantry battalions plus artillery, engineers and support troops. The known beach defences consisted of heavy bamboo stakes, some nine feet in diameter and 15 feet high. These were very firmly set to a depth of six feet into the sea bed in a straight line positioned just above the low water mark and spaced eight to ten feet apart. It was subsequently found by experiment that these obstructions were capable of resisting a ramming by a LCM with its bow door down.

3 Commando Brigade was placed under the command of 25th Indian Infantry Division (Major General G.N.Wood OBE, MC). The Brigade's role was to spearhead an amphibious assault and secure the immediate area including Myebon village (a small coastal township) and its jetty. The landings were timed to coincide with the high water mark: the timing was crucial if the troops were to gain a foothold on the beach.

Naval gunfire support was provided by the anti-aircraft cruiser HMS *Phoebe* and destroyers *Rapid, Raider, Pathfinder, Nepal, Napier,* the sloop HMS *Shoreham* and two Indian Navy sloops *Nabada* and *Jumna* (Rear Adml A.D.Read CB, RN). Air cover was provided by 224 Group RAF.

The assault landing on 12th January was preceded by a simultaneous naval bombardment and Allied air attack. Squadrons of fighter-bombers (Lightnings, Hurribombers, Thunderbolts and Spitfires) flew strafing runs over the landing areas. At the same time 36 Mitchell bombers attacked the area around Agnu village and other known enemy positions. To the Commandos poised and waiting in the landing craft off-shore, the whole peninsula appeared to lift up under the heavy air onslaught. On the night previous to the landing, a small party of swimmers/canoeists from the Combined Operations Assault Pilotage Party laid charges against the enemy beach defences set to detonate as the assault commenced. The timing was superb, several of the bamboo stakes were destroyed as the first landing craft approached the beaches. A gap was created through which the landing craft could navigate to reach the shoreline.

The Brigade, led by 42(RM) Commando went ashore from 12 LCMs and several minor craft under cover of a smoke screen laid from the air against fairly light opposition. The timely destruction of the beach defences took the enemy completely by surprise. One landing craft was hit by Japanese 75mm gunfire and several men were wounded by anti-personnel mines laid on the beach. These were the first such devices encountered since the Brigade had embarked on operations in Burma. 42 seized a beachhead enabling 5 to land and pass through the marines positions to continue the Brigade's advance towards Myebon. At this point the assault plan went sadly awry. It was the intention to land the second wave (1 and 44 Commandos) on an adjacent beach. A costly signalling mistake resulted in the landing craft carrying the two units to follow the same course as 5 and 42 Commando. 1 and 44 therefore landed on a muddy exposed beach, which at low tide was the natural habitat of crocodiles and snakes.

At 1130 hours 44 embarked into LCMs to be taken ashore. By the time the marines disembarked, the water was almost at its lowest ebb. The landing craft, despite their shallow draft, grounded approximately 400 yards from the beach. 44 stepped from their craft into waist high water and thick, glutinous grey mud. Marching across the Achnacarry heather during training, when a man's calf muscles screamed in agony was, by comparison, child's play. Hardly able to put one foot in front of the other through the knee high layer of mud which formed the sea bed, the marines toiled their way towards the beach. The mud claimed boots and socks, literally sucking them off men's feet as they moved forward at a snail's pace.

Some men fought individual battles; others formed rugby scrums to overcome the clinging morass beneath the water. When a scrum collapsed, it took several minutes for the marines to untangle themselves and their equipment, both men and weapons by now completely plastered in slimy sludge. As the weary men neared the beach they were pulled ashore through the steeply shelving final few yards by ropes thrown by their comrades on dry land. The thought of crocodiles and poisonous snakes was immaterial, nothing could compel 44's marines to move forward with more speed. By the time the unit had assembled on the beach, completely exhausted and covered in mud it had taken over two hours to cover the strength sapping quarter-mile from the landing craft to the shore.

Swimmer-canoeists of the Special Boat Section had carried out an undercover reconnaissance of the beach at the planning stage of the operation, and clearly identified the adverse conditions. However, Divisional Headquarters staff, in their wisdom, had concluded that the beach was firm throughout. This conclusion had been based on the study of aerial photographs!

The Commandos' superb physical condition and perseverance had averted a hazardous situation from becoming something much worse. After cleaning their weapons the Commando moved off, initially to take over the beach defence responsibility from 42. As 44's marines settled into their defensive positions they discovered not only military stores, but an abundance of tinned salmon left behind by the Japanese, uncharacteristically free of any booby-trap devices.

13th January:

During the night the marines heard firing from the area where 1 Commando was known to be operating. With the coming of daylight 44's marines discovered yet more booty, including quantities of food and military equipment. An infantry brigade was landed to follow up the Commando Brigade. At 1000 hours 44 moved away from the beachhead towards Myebon village. With a company of mules carrying an additional section of 3-inch mortars (Ox and Bucks Light Infantry) under command, the unit moved forward in direct support of their 42 colleagues as they attacked the hill feature code-named 'Cabbage.' Although the hill was successfully captured without incurring any fatal casualties 42's CO (Lt Col H.D.Fellowes) was wounded during the action. For the first time the Commandos worked in unison with Sherman tanks of the 19th Indian Lancers. The marines boxed close to the coastline north of Myebon, to spend a cold and uncomfortable night in the jungle, the situation aggravated by the acute shortage of rations.

14th January:

In the early hours of the morning sentries sighted a sampan carrying enemy soldiers in the Myebon River. The craft was bearing down on 44's positions, probably attracted by the noise of braying mules. The craft was engaged by HMIS *Nabada* and destroyed. Early the following morning 44 were targeted by an enemy 75mm gun, all the rounds fired fell to the south of where the marines were dug-in. Later on 44 moved a short distance across country to join 1 Commando on the hill code-named Onion, which had been captured by the Army Commandos on the previous day. A water party from 44 was shelled by a 75mm gun as they approached a nearby village. Fortunately no casualties were sustained. The shortage of rations still remained a problem and foraging for food, especially eggs became a major preoccupation. The CO received word that the Brigade would launch a series of attacks on the surrounding hills sometime during the next day. In the early afternoon the marines witnessed an aerial bombardment of the intended targets by Allied aircraft. 44's allotted task would be to wait for 1 to take their objective, Hill 200, before passing through the Army Commando's lines to seize the next objective, Hill 163.

15th January:

The Commando moved to the start line at 0830 to await the capture of Hill 200. The order for 44 to commence their attack came at 1150 hours and the marines moved across open paddy fields towards their objective. Supported by the 19th Lancers' tanks, the advance was made under cover of both a planned smoke screen plus the smoke from the paddy fields set ablaze by the the 3-inch mortars and type 77 grenades. The Japanese beat a hasty retreat in the face of 44's determined attack and by 1320 hours all the heavily bunkered enemy positions had been captured. Casualties had been confined to one man wounded, a sergeant in A Tp. During the advance, a section of B Tp had overrun a portion of an adjacent hill (Bugle): only to be withdrawn when 5 made representations to the effect that the marines were on 'their' hill.

The Brigade's leap-frog tactics continued. After 44 had passed through 1 to gain their objective, both 5 and 42 passed through 44's lines to attack hills closer to the final objective, the village of Kantha. As darkness approached the unit boxed for the night in the area around Hill 163. X Tp discovered an abandoned enemy bunker within their defence perimeter containing various maps and other documents. These papers provided detailed Japanese strengths and the defensive locations of enemy troops on the peninsula. This excellent intelligence information was retrieved only after the bunker had been cleared of several booby traps. The marines were subjected to spasmodic sniper fire throughout the night hours without taking any casualties. All in all the Commando had had a good day which was rounded off with a welcome issue of the infamous 'Rosa' rum. Firewater to drink, this spirit, used in conjunction with a round cigarette tin and a boot lace, produced a very acceptable level of illumination.

16th January:

The marines spent a quiet day on and around Hill 163. A jeep was purloined and together with the assistance of local porters the unit received an adequate supply of essential stores and a delivery of mail. Patrols were sent out during the day. A section from C Tp (Lt Owen) returned with a large cache of trophies including weapons and a pair of periscope binoculars while Capt Hamlin (X Tp) patrolled as far as the village of Gaungpyu where a box of Japanese military documents was found. These papers were later forwarded to the Brigade's intelligence officers for closer scrutiny.

17th January:

The captured documents included maps indicating Japanese defensive positions on the mainland between Myebon and Kangaw. Lt A.P.O'Brien MC, with a patrol from C Tp was given the task of landing on the west bank of the Myebon River to probe forward to establish the extent of these enemy defences. Following a night river passage north by landing craft, the patrol was put ashore before dawn in an area close to the village of Chaunggyi. The information gathered would be vital to the planning of the next stage of the operation: the capture of Kangaw.

During the day Major H.F.C.Kimpton joined the Commando as 2i/c. His predecessor, Major H.G.S.Saunders was transferred to Brigade HQ, subsequently taking command of the forward supply base at Teknaf. Before he left the unit Major Saunders compiled a list of essential stores required by 44.

18th January:

During the night the marines of 44 could hear the sounds of battle to the north of Kantha. It was later learned that two separate enemy counter-attacks had been repulsed by Allied units operating to the north of the Commando Brigade's positions. Later in the day 44 received instructions to divide and relocate its rifle troops. A Tp was immediately moved to Kantha Bridge, the river crossing separating the Myebon Peninsula from the mainland. The next day C and X Tps, plus Major Kimpton and a small HQ set off to join Lt O'Brien's patrol which had established itself in Netthitke village. B Tp with Commando HQ relocated to Kantha village relieving a battalion of 74 Brigade.

19th January:

The relocation of the rifle troops commenced at 0800 hours, B Tp and HQ moving off towards Kantha where they arrived 45 minutes later. Lt Col Stockley watched as C and X Tps embarked in landing craft, manned by fellow Royal Marines, for the trip up the Myebon River to join Lt O'Brien and his party. No sooner had 44 been redeployed than the CO received instructions to recall his marines and move the unit back to Agnu village for a short rest. The Brigade was to spearhead another amphibious assault: Kangaw.

20th January:

The day proved to be one of hectic activity. The Adjutant moved post-haste to Agnu to make arrangements for the unit's imminent arrival. A Tp and Commando HQ arrived together at 1145 hours. B Tp remained at Kantha Bridge awaiting relief by elements of 74 Brigade. C and X Tps rejoined the unit at Agnu in the early afternoon, bringing with them a very sick Major Kimpton. The 2i/c had been struck down by an acute bout of malaria which necessitated immediate hospitalisation. During the short time spent at Netthitke the two Troops (C and X) had discovered several empty Japanese defensive positions linked by field telephones. Before leaving the area, telephone wires were cut and the hand sets thrown into the chaung. The marines also brought back three Chin tribesmen who were able to pass on valuable local information to the intelligence section relevant to the coming operation. The Commando received a second batch of mail and bedrolls were sent up from the rear. Small fires and smoking were allowed during the dark hours and everyone settled down to get a good nights rest before the Brigade pulled out the following afternoon.

21st January:

The Brigade Commander congratulated Lt O'Brien's patrol for providing the information which had proved to be essential to the planning of the forthcoming operation. The morning was spent preparing weapons and equipment in readiness for the coming operation. At 1300 hours 44 formed up by troops to march down to the beach to embark in waiting landing craft. The marines were ferried out to the LCIs which were to carry them down the coast and up the Daignbon Chaung to the landing beach at Kangaw.

The Kangaw Blockade
22nd January-2nd February 1945

The Allied forces in the Arakan were steadily pushing an estimated Japanese force of over 5,000 men and guns (including at least one 150mm artillery piece) southwards. The recent capture of Myebon had effectively cut the enemy water-borne escape routes to the sea down through the numerous chaungs. The only remaining through route left open was the Myohaung-Tamandu road. The village of Kangaw

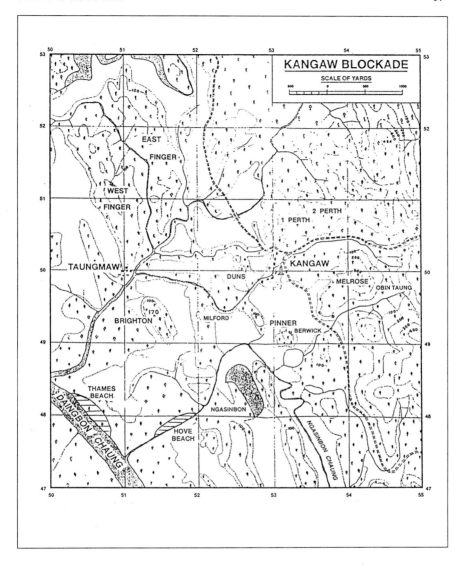

straddles the road, lying eight miles north-east of Myebon. Kangaw was destined to become the stage for the bloodiest battle fought during the Allies struggle to conquer the Arakan region. 3 Commando Brigade was to play a decisive role in the action. The defence of the infamous Hill 170 earned for the Brigade a posthumous Victoria Cross, two Distinguished Service Orders, two Distinguished Conduct Medals, numerous Military Crosses (officers), Military Medals (other ranks) plus several other awards and accolades from all quarters.

Lt Gen Christison (GOC XV Indian Corps) realised that by cutting the road at Kangaw the Japanese army in the Arakan would be cut in half. Not unexpectedly the enemy appreciated the strategic importance of the road. The artillery in the hills to the north and east gave the enemy dominance over the road and surrounding area. Any Allied headway through the hills from the north would be a time consuming operation with the numerous chaungs forming natural barriers to a rapid advance. Time was of the essence, the capture of Kangaw would only be possible if achieved before massive enemy reinforcements could be brought up from the south. A surprise attack required to be mounted as a matter of urgency, the problem was from which direction! Most of the Japanese defences were geared to repel an attack from the north. A bold strategy was developed by the planning staff of 25 Indian Division and 3 Commando Brigade to land an attacking force from the Daingbon chaung at a point two miles to the south-west of the village followed by an aggressive advance from this, an unexpected quarter.

The designated landing areas lay between two unnamed chaungs running into the main Daingbon Chuang. The main beach-head was on the east bank of the Daingbon, codenamed Thames. A smaller landing area from the lower unnamed chaung was code-named Hove. 'Beach' is a misnomer, the Arakan chaungs in general offered few recognisable landing places. The beach was little more than a convenient gap in the mangrove swamp, mangrove being a tangle of submerged tree roots, rotting foliage and mud, with the adjacent areas unexpectedly swamped at high water. At low tide the mangrove remained exposed, making progress on foot, over the mass of wet tangled vegetation extremely difficult. The terrain made it impossible to land wheeled vehicles of any description. All supplies, fresh water and ammunition required manhandling from the beach up to the point of use. The shortage of drinking water presented a serious and ongoing problem.

The beach-head was almost an island, being surrounded on three sides by chaungs. The direct land approach from the beach to Kangaw would entail the Brigade initially clearing Hill 170 (codenamed Brighton) of enemy forces known to be established on the feature. The hill was approximately 700 yards long, 300 yards wide and 100 feet high, surrounded on all sides by paddy fields or mangrove swamp. Between Hill 170 and the village lay a strategically positioned hill running almost north-south, codenamed Pinner. Another smaller hill, Milford, lay between the two. The distance between Pinner and Hill 170 was approximately 1200 yards, the beach a further mile to the south-west of '170.' The battle plan required that the entire Commando Brigade, plus an attached battalion of Indian infantry (8/10 Hyderabads) to land and concentrate in a rough square measuring two miles in each direction.

In the course of the coming 12 days the four Commando units would become so intermingled during the fighting that Kangaw would truly be seen as a Brigade action. The Brigade would be supported by a battery of 25-pdr guns mounted on Z Lighters (large flat-topped, self-propelled barges) anchored in the Daingbon chaung. The two Royal Indian Navy sloops *Jumna* and *Nabada* would provide naval gunfire support. After clearing Hill 170 the Brigade would move forward towards Kangaw to capture the neighbouring hills (Milford and Pinner). With these objectives secured, 51 Indian Infantry Brigade[13] would land, moving through the Commandos' positions to launch attacks on hills codenamed Duns, Berwick, Perth (1 and 2) and Melrose. The occupation of the high ground overlooking the road would result in a complete block on the enemy escape route south.

The assault plan was daring in concept: the prize, to catch the enemy defending Kangaw unprepared and exposed. The element of surprise was fundamental to the success of the plan. A flotilla of 50 ships and other craft (minesweepers, motor launches and assorted landing craft) supported by HMIS *Nabada*, were required to navigate a course taking the vessels 27 miles inland; the last 18 miles of the journey through winding, unpredictable narrow chaungs and mangrove swamp in broad daylight.

The price to be paid for surprise, the convoy would converge on the chosen landing area without the support of preliminary air attacks, naval or artillery bombardment. Air bombardment was synchronized to commence as the Commandos landed. No. 224 Group, RAF would provide maximum air support throughout the operation. In addition to the British and Commonwealth airmen, the Air Group was augmented by four squadrons of American B25 Mitchell bombers and B24 Liberator bombers of the Strategic Air Force.

---

13   51 Brigade was the first 'all Indian' Brigade. All other Indian Infantry Brigades contained two Indian and one or two British battalions.

22nd January:

Enemy guns commenced firing as the first landing craft neared the beach at 1245 hours. Undeterred, 1 Commando, leading the assault, landed under cover of smoke laid by Allied aircraft. The marines of 44 went ashore at 1500 hours, in the first instance deploying in the beach area, acting as the Brigade reserve. Two hours later 44 moved forward, concentrating at the rear of Hill 170, most of which had been cleared by 1 at the cost of three dead and nine wounded. The marines awaited nightfall before advancing to attack Milford. Minus A & S Tps (beach defence), they reached the objective against little opposition and proceeded to dig-in. During the night the enemy mounted a probing attack on '170' where the bulk of the Brigade was established. 44's position came under attack at the same time and the unit sustained its first casualties of the action, two marines of X Tp receiving fatal wounds.

23rd January:

Shortly after first light C Tp advanced, unopposed, to Pinner: the remainder of the Commando followed on throughout the morning. By early afternoon the unit, now including A & S Tps, was digging-in on the hill. The hill although approximately the same height as '170' was considerably smaller (300 yards long by 100 yards wide), with steep jungle-covered slopes. The Commando was now the most forward unit of the Brigade and nearest to Kangaw village.

A small patrol provided by B Tp proceeded first to the next hill (Berwick) and then to the road south of the village. No enemy movement was seen. Lt Col Stockley received orders to continue hill-hopping. The next objective was Duns, a hill one mile to the north of Pinner. To reach the hill entailed crossing the chaung forming the northern boundary of the beachhead. At 1730 hours Lt Bayliss and two volunteers set off to reconnoitre a route for the advance planned to start at 0200 hours. Moving across the surrounding paddy fields the small party came under fire from an enemy machine gun, the trio escaped unscathed and pushed on to reach Duns. As the three marines arrived at the objective a 75mm gun opened fire, again all the men escaped injury and returned to the unit at 1830 hours.

The Japanese were by now mindful of the danger that 3 Commando Brigade presented. Despite being out-manoeuvred by the unexpected landing, the enemy was to subject the Commandos to counter-attacks, the ferocity of which was unsurpassed. 44 had the dubious honour of experiencing the first large-scale attack.

Following the usual dusk 'stand to' 44 settled down to watch and wait. The area on and around Pinner, bathed in bright moonlight, presented an eerie and almost unnatural landscape. The general sense of unease, the forbidding surroundings and feelings of apprehension combined to create an atmosphere thick enough to have been cut with a knife. 'Royal' did not have long to wait!

At around 2000 hours, enemy artillery registered the marines' position on Pinner, the shelling being the prelude to a whole night of savage fighting. Shortly before midnight Japanese field guns had been joined by heavy machine guns and mortars. The intense firepower shredded the tree covered hill-top, shell fragments and large, razor sharp wood splinters causing several early casualties. The guns fired almost point-blank into 44's positions, the muzzle flashes being instantaneously followed by exploding shells.

This was a different breed of artilleryman to those encountered at Alethangyaw. On Pinner the noise was deafening, shells were hitting the marines positions accurately and rapidly, the air reeked of cordite and vast dust clouds hung suspended in the humid air.

The initial barrage was quickly followed by the first infantry attack. A party of enemy soldiers advanced through the thick foliage in front of 44's forward positions and were engaged by the nearest Bren-gun teams. The first wave was repelled and in the period of quiet following the engagement, the cries and groans of the Japanese wounded and the popping of water bottle corks could clearly be heard coming from the paddy field at the base of the hill. The marines waited in silence for the next attack, and the next, and the next. Throughout the night the Japanese were relentless in attack, on occasions the fanatical forward thrust of their advance carried the enemy infantrymen into the rain of fire being put down by their own gunners. Machine guns and mortars supporting the enemy assault inflicting a heavy stream of casualties on the Commando.

In the short periods of calm between attacks, the enemy would call out for help in English as they had done at Alethangyaw. 'Johnny I'm wounded, over here.' The marines, wise to the ploy did not respond. The enemy began using grenade launchers, the grenades landing in and around the Commando's trenches causing casualties wherever they fell. The marines responded in kind, rolling grenades down the hill among the attackers.

An enemy mortar was set up in the paddy field, close enough to the defenders for them to hear the fire orders being shouted in Japanese. The unit's Bren-gunners maintained a withering fire to repel repeated enemy charges. The light machine guns' two man crews were prime targets and the marines operating the Bren-guns sustained several casualties during the night. The Brens proved crucial during the prolonged assaults against the marines. To maintain the firepower the guns provided, empty magazines were refilled with rounds taken from riflemen's bandoliers.

The marines' fire discipline was superb, the conservation of ammunition being paramount. Although the enemy could be heard in the paddy fields below, the marines only fired when a target was clearly seen. It was impossible to evacuate the wounded from the hilltop during the action: casualties having to wait until daylight before being removed. As the night wore on the Japanese tactics changed. Direct advances up the hill with machine gun and mortar support were being consistantly thwarted by the marines. The enemy commander, realising that 44 would not succumb to this type of attack began to send small parties of infantrymen to infiltrate through the marines' positions. On occasions the Commandos were forced into hand-to-hand combat, using the bayonet, the Commando fighting knife, rifle butts, fists, heads, knees and booted feet before the attackers were driven back. The only intruder who managed to worm through 44's defences was a large, shell-shocked, porcupine. The unfortunate rodent scrambled into a trench alongside the RSM. There followed a brief altercation between the two before the porcupine moved on to find more amenable company. The RSM was left to extract several quills from his nether regions.

Before dawn 44 was subjected to another series of mortar, machine gun and infantry attacks, all of which were repelled. Daylight revealed the first evidence of the battle with the dead and wounded littering the hilltop and its slopes. Every man in the unit was utterly exhausted: most losing good friends in the battle. The Commando lost 20 dead and over 40 seriously wounded. Capt A.Martin, the signals officer and one of the original 3RM officers died of his wounds.

By holding Pinner on only the second night of the campaign, 44 prevented the Japanese from establishing a firm base on the hill from which to bombard the other Commando units on Hill 170 less than a mile away. Until additional units landed, 3 Commando Brigade's task was to hold the beachhead, and 44's stand had shown the Japanese that the Commando soldiers would not be easily shifted.

24th January:

At 0900 hours Brig Hardy visited 44's hilltop positions. Shortly afterwards the Commando received orders to make ready for relief by the battalion of 8/10 Hyderabads which came forward later in the day. Fresh rations arrived, allowing all ranks to eat a good meal, for some the first food taken since landing. Advance parties from the Hyderabads arrived throughout the morning prior to the change over. Before 44 left Pinner, the Chaplain conducted the burial service for those members of the Commando killed during the previous nights action. The simple service was attended by marines from A and C Tps plus members of the rear HQ. Once relieved the Commando moved back to Hill 170 and by the middle of the afternoon the marines were busy digging trenches on its north-west slope.

Even though the unit was in the middle of an operation, the administrative wheels of the Brigade kept turning and for three lucky individuals, 28 days leave in the UK! The necessary ballots brought forth the winners: Lt Owen (C Tp), Sgt C.Barrett (HQ Tp) and Mne Knowles (X Tp). All three left the unit the following day.

Signals Troop. Troop leader Capt A. Martin (killed at Kangaw) front row, centre.

25th January:

During the morning Lt Col Stockley attended a conference at Brigade HQ, returning with the news that the Commando would remain in its present location, sending out fighting patrols when ordered. 44 was positioned between 1 Commando's 4 Tp and Heavy Weapons Tp. With the two units intermingled the soldiers and marines jointly planned the defence of the immediate area, conspiring together to construct lethal booby traps 'for the use of.'

26th January:

Enemy artillery bracketed '170' in the early hours, 44's positions receiving a 30 minute battering during which two marines of S Tp were killed and Lt.W.W.Brydon and a marine of X Tp wounded. The shelling resumed at 0630 although the Commando escaped any casualties. After breakfast the Commandos had a grandstand view of Allied aircraft attacking enemy positions in the hills surrounding Kangaw village. During the morning 44 moved off Hill 170 to take over the defence of the two beaches (A and C Tps) and the two chaungs: the northern chaung, X Tp; the southern chaung, B Tp. With HQ set up to the west of Thames beach the unit's rifle troops were spread over the whole Brigade area. X Tp, arriving at their positions to defend the northern chaung, came under artillery fire: one marine was killed and six others wounded. During the day the Commando Brigade received welcome reinforcements when the rest of 51 Indian Infantry Brigade plus tanks of 19th Lancers arrived, moving forward to relieve the units holding Pinner and Melrose. The Indian Brigade's task was to set up the block on the road heading south and await the arrival of 53 and 74 Brigades who were advancing towards Kangaw overland from Myebon.

27th January:

The Japanese early morning bombardment concentrated on A and C Tps defending the beach area, over 50 incoming rounds were counted within a period of 30 minutes. The marines' trenches were by now 'half way down to Australia' and no casualties were sustained during the barrage. The rest of the Brigade redeployed around Hill 170. X Tp joined 5 on the hill whilst maintaining a 24 hour standing patrol of the northern chaung. The Brigadier was everywhere, talking to the marines and soldiers, relating the current situation and what he thought would be the likely enemy strategy. With X Tp spread out between '170' and the northern chaung, 42 took over responsibility for the standing patrol.

The four Commando units had by now become totally intermixed. As every man wore an identical green beret (minus any regimental cap badge) the Brigade was seen, uniquely, as a single fighting force.

In the afternoon Capt Macan led a mixed patrol (A and B Tps) sent to engage an enemy force of between 50 and 60 reported to be in the village of Kyauktan. Meanwhile intelligence reports indicated that the Brigade was likely to come under attack during the night. Capt Macan's patrol was immediately recalled to booster the Brigade's defences before they could complete their allotted task. Before being recalled the marines found a British 2-pdr gun and a Boys anti-tank rifle, owners unknown! On '170' X Tp received a visit from the Deputy Brigade Commander. Col Young brought news that the Tp would move to new positions during the night. The expected enemy assault did not materialise. However, X Tp were on the receiving end of shelling, one marine being wounded.

28th January:

Throughout the day the Brigade's positions were subjected to continual artillery salvos, an estimated 1000 shells landing in the restricted area of the beachhead. The barrage was considered to be the heaviest concentration of fire delivered against the Allies throughout the whole Burma campaign. 44's patrol activity to the far side of the northern tidal chaung was always subject to minute timing: at high water the chaung became impassable. A small patrol (Sgt A.J.Webber) reached Gnasinbon North. Although no enemy soldiers were seen, it was clear that the village was being used as a supply point by the Japanese. A silence followed the day of incessant bombardment, allowing the unit to enjoy a comparatively quiet night free from shelling.

29th January:

Patrolling continued throughout the day with the local population providing an abundance of useful information which was swiftly acted upon. One patrol (Lt Henshall) was dispatched to locate and destroy two anti-tank guns seen in the surrounding hills by local natives. The marines set out at 0900 hours. After successfully locating the two guns, the armaments were destroyed with explosives and the ammunition dumped into a nearby chaung. Other patrols gathered information concerning enemy strengths and positions. A section from B Tp (Capt Sturges) reached Ngasinbon South to find the village partly destroyed by fire. No contact was made with the enemy.

During the afternoon all elements of the Commando came together for the first time for some days to set up positions around Daingbon village. Intelligence reports indicated that a large body of escaping enemy troops would attempt to cross the Daingbon chaung sometime during the night. At 2130 hours an ambush party (Capt Macan) embarked into landing craft, leaving the Commando area to mount a night attack, only to discover from local inhabitants that the Japanese force had passed through an hour before the marines' arrival.

30th January:

Most of the smaller hills surrounding Kangaw village were by now occupied by 51 Indian Infantry Brigade, with 3 Commando Brigade defending the crucial landing beaches and Hill 170. The Japanese were fighting furiously to regain the ground lost to the Allied forces. During the early hours 44's marines heard a heavy enemy attack being mounted against Melrose. The Commando spent a quiet day waiting for the expected battle to develop.

As the Indian Brigades were being supplied from the beach through the Commando Brigade's lines, Hill 170 was the key to the whole operation. The Japanese commander decided to commit his troops, drawn from the renowned Matsu Detachment, to an all-out assault on '170.' If he could dislodge the Commandos and occupy the hill, the supply route to the forward Allied troops presently occupying the hills overlooking his escape route south would be cut. A subsequent Allied withdrawal from the high ground would allow the Japanese to reopen the north/south escape route.

31st January:

When the Japanese launched the heaviest and most desperate counter-attack in the early hours of the morning, 1 and 42 were occupying the defensive positions on Hill 170. The enemy, desperate to capture the feature mounted a fanatical assault, irrespective of casualties. The sheer weight of numbers thrown at the defenders dictated that some positions would be over-run. Enemy assault engineers destroyed two out of three tanks (19 Lancers) caught laagered in a sheltered position; the third tank broke clear to decimate the attacking enemy force. The battle for possession of the hill continued, Japanese artillery preventing any units of the Indian Infantry Brigades being moved back across the open paddy fields to reinforce the Commandos on and around Hill 170. Elements of 5 were, however, sent to reinforce the defenders during the night to be followed by 44's A, X and S Tps during the morning. The tactics used by the Japanese were almost identical to those used against 44 on Pinner eight days earlier.

During the engagement Lt G.Knowland (1 Commando) won a posthumous Victoria Cross. The Brigade stood fast on the hill. When the enemy finally withdrew they left over 350 dead behind. During the twelve day battle for Kangaw, 3 Commando Brigade lost 86 killed (27 from 44) and approximately 250 wounded (60 from 44). The Army and

Royal Marines Commandos exhibited to the full the inherent qualities of tenacity, temperament and thoroughness in everything they were ordered to do during the action. With the exception of 44, the Brigade was relieved later in the day by Indian troops (7/16 Punjabis), allowing 1, 5 and 42 to return to Myebon.

1st February:

After this, the final battle for '170,' there was little enemy activity. During the respite the RSM and two marines placed crosses on the graves of dead comrades buried on Hills 170 and Pinner. Lt Col Stockley gathered the unit together, telling the men of the esteem in which the Commando was held, emanating from the way in which the marines tenaciously held on to Pinner shortly after the Brigade landed. The CO expected the unit to be relieved the next day, allowing 44 to rejoin the remainder of the Brigade at Myebon.

In Lord Louis Mountbatten's opinion, the operation was an outstanding example of inter-service co-operation. The Royal Navy, in direct support of the land forces had the responsibility for providing the stores, equipment and medical services necessary to sustain the soldiers and marines in the field. A Field Surgical Unit was embarked on board HMIS *Narbada*. Minesweepers were utilised to serve as hospital carriers and landing craft doubled as casualty clearing stations, water carriers and supply vessels. The Spitfires, Hurricanes and Thunderbolts of the Allied air forces continually strafed and bombed the Kangaw road and hill positions held by the enemy. Between 26th January and 2nd February USAAF Liberator and Mitchell bombers dropped 750 tons of bombs on the Japanese forces.

The Battle of Kangaw, although not receiving the same news coverage, was comparable to the other great actions fought in Burma: Kohima, Imphal and the Administrative Box (Kalapanzin valley).

The Japanese losses included 2000 men killed plus 16 guns and 14 large motor craft destroyed. The Allied casualties, British, Indian and Gurkha, were recorded as 600 killed and wounded.

Praise was heaped on the Brigade from all directions: Lord Louis Mountbatten was reported to have been ecstatic on hearing of the Brigade's monumental struggle to successfully defend Hill 170 and the surrounding areas against a determined enemy. Newspaper reporters queued up for information and the Brigade received complete sets of replacement uniforms from XV Indian Corps almost immediately after the Commandos returned to Myebon. The highest accolades were contained in 'Special Order of the Day' messages from the Corps Commander, XV Indian Corps and from the General Officer

Commanding, 25th Indian Division.

Lt.Gen Sir A.F.Philip Christison KBE, CB, MC, commanding XV Indian Corps:

> Having been placed under command of 15 Ind Corps to lead assaults in particularly hazardous and important amphibious operations, you have successfully completed the tasks which were assigned to you.
>
> Your courage and determination in assault and attacks, your tenacity and aggressiveness in defence and counter attack have won the praise and admiration of the Commanders and Troops, British, Indian and Gurkha of all other formations engaged in the operations and who have fought beside you. Through your exploits at AKYAB, MYEBON and KANGAW and the valuable reconnaissances which you made along the Arakan Coast, you have gained a reputation throughout the Corps for indifference to personal danger, for ruthless pursuit in success, for resourceful determination in adversity, which has been a source of inspiration to your Comrades in Arms.
>
> The Battle of KANGAW has been the decisive battle of the the whole Arakan Campaign and that it was won was very largely due to your magnificent defence of Hill 170.
>
> I am very proud of you and thank you for the decisive contribution which you have made to the success of the Campaign and the rout of the Jap in this theatre of operations.
>
> I deplore the loss of your gallant Comrades and I trust that your wounded may soon be restored to your ranks.
>
> For the future, I wish you all happiness and success.

And from Maj. Gen G.N.Wood OBE, MC, commander 25th Indian Division:

> On the victorious conclusion of the operations for the capture of the MYEBON Peninsula and the cutting of the enemy lines of communication at KANGAW, I wish, on behalf of 25 Ind Div to express to 3 Commando Brigade the admiration we feel for their support and fire in attack, and their aggressive and cheerful spirit when defensive actions have been imposed upon them. Three Commando Brigade has had a stern test - for many officers and men their baptism of fire - but have emerged from it with a

reputation of which all ranks must always be proud. Their comrades of 25 Ind Div deplore their losses among them many who had already become our personal friends, but these losses have been avenged in full.

I count not least among the fruits of victory the mutual trust and esteem which has been established on the battlefield between the soldiers of 3 Commando Brigade and their British and especially their Indian Comrades of 25 Ind Div.

Myebon
2nd-18th February 1945

The Commando boarded a flotilla of assorted landing craft in the early afternoon of 2nd February for the two hour trip back to Myebon. As a farewell gesture enemy gunners fired a 150mm round into the beach area which landed 30 yards from where the marines were embarking. The unit returned to the Myebon Peninsula landing at Easy Beach at 1615 hours. The Commando formed up by troops to march back to rejoin the Brigade in an area south of the village. 44 marched into the camp with as much swank as they could muster 45 minutes after setting off. 44's marines found a hot meal and rum issue waiting for them, plus bed rolls and most important of all, mail!

Following a night's rest the Commando received an informal visit from Brig Hardy, who complimented 44 on the effort put in during the past twelve days of continuous action at Kangaw. He told the unit that the Brigade would stay in Myebon for approximately ten days, after which the future was uncertain. It was unlikely that the Brigade would be earmarked for further large scale operations, although it was possible that 44 would be used to provide small raiding parties, functioning in the true commando role of mounting lightning attacks against enemy targets along the Arakan coastline.

The following five days were spent re-equipping the unit, sorting out the troops and catching up on personal administration. The unit had lost close to 20% of its personnel killed and wounded during the recent action. The casualty list created imbalances within the unit, resulting in some men being transferred between troops to attain a balanced Commando once more. On 4th February the CO assembled his marines to formally read the list of casualties sustained during the action at Kangaw.

The next day the Brigade paraded before Major General G.N.Wood (commander 25th Indian Infantry Division). The General's wholesome praise was followed by the promulgation of a Special Order of the Day. Every man received a complete new issue of 'jungle greens,' signalling a resumption of warlike activities. The period 9th-18th February saw 44 divided into two groups to undertake several minor operations around Myebon.

Edward Force (B & C Tps):

The first task allocated to Edward Force was to provide protection to a 25-pdr gun battery located along the coast. A vigilant sentry, standing night guard in a position overlooking one of the many chaungs in the area caused a few eyebrows to be raised when he suddenly reported the approach of a Japanese midget submarine. His somewhat sceptical Troop Leader crept warily forward through the jungle to investigate this very bizarre sighting. The captain of marines was gratified to discover that the enemy had not developed a deadly secret amphibious weapon. However, the officer concerned was then less than impressed to find that his careful and unseen approach had brought him to within snapping distance of a very large, unfriendly crocodile.

Routine patrols were sent out into the surrounding area without coming into contact with any enemy units. Japanese counter-battery fire became very predictable. In the early evening on both 12th and 14th February enemy artillery probed the Edward Force positions. On both days 30 shells were fired, the incoming rounds landed harmlessly some 500-700 yards from the Allied battery guarded by 'Royal.' During this activity, Lt Col Stockley arrived with a small HQ team to take over command. Lt Musters led patrols to two nearby villages without coming across any evidence of enemy activity. As the CO, Commando HQ and B Tp relocated to provide protection to a second Royal Artillery gun battery, the marines were recalled; the Commando was placed on 24 hours notice to move to Akyab. The detachment was immediately transported back to Myebon by landing craft, arriving on 18th February.

Bert Force (A, X and HQ Tps):

On 9th February the detachment was ferried by landing craft out to LCI 296 lying at anchor off Myebon. The vessel subsequently provided a floating base from which LCAs put recce patrols ashore at several points along the coastline. The marines were able to provide useful intelligence on likely sites suitable for air-strips and gun positions, plus the available water supply and the condition of roads and beaches. This information was used to plan future operations by other units.

A small detachment was detailed to provide protection for HMIS *Nabada*, moored at the mouth of the Thayettaung chaung.

At 0200 hours, 12th February a patrol led by Capt Watkins (A Tp) landed from LCI 296 to shoot up a party of enemy troops believed to be in a local village. As the marines approached their objective, they were seen by three enemy soldiers who made off in great haste, two men leaving all their kit behind as they made a hurried escape. LCI 296 returned to Myebon on the 13th February and the marines were transferred back to 'Easy' beach. The men marched back to the Brigade area, only to discover that the whole detachment was to be placed in immediate quarantine. An Indian Army doctor attached to Bert Force had contracted Smallpox, thus involving all ranks receiving a precautionary vaccination as a matter of urgency. The necessary arrangements made, 'Royal' spent the night in isolation to await the 'jab.' Everyone's spirits were raised when it became known that beer and canteen stores were available to the men in quarantine. Mne Norman (A Tp) was happier than most; he had been selected to take 28 days leave in the UK.

Akyab
19th February-14th March 1945

The three weeks 44 spent back at Akyab were used to recoup after six weeks of continuous operations. The Commando departed from Myebon on Z Lighters, arriving at Akyab during the early evening. After going ashore the marines climbed onto motor transport for the onward journey to a camp established at Donbyin where 44 had been briefly billeted following the initial landings on 3rd January. On arrival the marines were greeted by a new Regimental Sergeant Major (WO1 Spencer) and the news that they would be sleeping in tents situated among a stand of trees. On the plus side the men were welcomed with a hot meal and received the all important mail from home.

The unit quickly settled into routine camp life. In addition to individual troop parades and weapon inspections, the Commando paraded for an official inspection by the brigade commander. Brig Hardy congratulated the CO on the standard of the marines' turn-out and precision as they marched past his saluting dais in column of threes.

Lt Gen Christison paid a visit to the Commando, emphasising the decisive role played by the Commando Brigade in the operations at

Myebon and Kangaw.

On 1st March the entire unit assembled for the CO to read the list of decorations won by members of the Commando at Alethangyaw.

Military Medal
Troop Sergeant Major G.M.Kemsley (A Tp)

Mentioned in Despatches
Capt A.Martin (Killed in action: Kangaw)
Capt E.M.Sturges (B Tp)
Lt A.R.White (Intelligence Officer)
Corporal T.W.Pemberton (Intelligence Section)
Corporal W.E.Lavender (X Tp)

44's sergeants' mess. TSM George Kemsley MM front row, extreme left.

At the same time, official photographs taken during Operation Screwdriver were made available for purchase.

As time slipped by 'Royal' set about, as always, improving the living conditions. Basha huts, all built to individual needs and specifications replaced tents. Although a basha could be made weatherproof, no in-built protection could be incorporated to prevent the local wildlife sharing the accommodation. 44's doctor received a nasty shock when he found a large Cobra in his basha.

Sporting contests were organized and social visits made to surrounding units. Reciprocal visits were made between 44 and the

8/10th Hyderabads who had relieved the Commando on 'Pinner.' Enormous curry dinners were eaten and washed down with liberal quantities of rum. Friendly games of football were played and wrestling competitions staged. With regular mail drops, beer in the canteen and sport, 44 felt quite content. Artistes attached to ENSA put on several shows for the troops billeted in and around Akyab, Francis Day, Patrica Burke and Wee Georgie Wood all appeared at the Garrison Theatre. The rest period came to an end with the news that the Brigade was to return to Bangalore: within 24 hours the destination had been changed to Nasik (100 miles north-east of Bombay). On 14th March the Commando Brigade boarded the LSI(L) *Dunera* for the first leg of the journey back across the Bay of Bengal to Madras.

Sea Time IV
Akyab to Madras
15th-18th March 1945

The *Dunera* was a purpose built troopship constructed at the Barclay Curle yard on the Clyde in 1937. Unfortunately for 3 Commando Brigade the *Dunera* had been converted to the role of Landing Ship Infantry (Large) in 1942! A squat, single funnelled, powerful looking vessel of 11,162 tons with a service speed of 14 knots, the ship was operated by British India Steam Navigation Co. Prior to the vessel's conversion to LSI(L) the *Dunera* had been 'trooping' (1939-41). In the new role the ship had taken part in the Sicily Landings in 1943 and in August 1944 was designated Headquarters Ship, US 7th Army during the campaign in the South of France. The vessel was dispatched to Far Eastern waters and after conveying the Commando Brigade to India, was engaged in the operations mounted to reoccupy Rangoon. The Commandos enjoyed the three day sea passage. With the exception of the customary periods of physical training the soldiers and marines relaxed, taking in the sea air and sunshine.

The men of 44 were among a select group of Royal Marines to be issued with the American M-1 Garand rifle. Although many infantry units of the 14th 'Army took delivery of the weapon, Royal Marines were a long way down the list. Only the nature of the Brigade's 'special service' field of operations ensured the issue of the Garand to the marine Commandos. The M-1 was a rifle with a well-deserved reputation, comparable to the British .303 Lee Enfield. The .30 Garand was a semi-automatic weapon weighing 9 lbs. With an overall length of 44 inches and bullets contained in clips of eight, the rifle, with its rapid rate of fire became a favoured weapon with 44's riflemen. The Garand also became the standard issue rifle to the entire United States Infantry. The flamboyant American General, George Patton described it as 'the greatest battle implement ever devised.' In anticipation of the expected issue of Garands to 44, RSM Spencer conducted a series of training sessions for SNCOs during the voyage across the Bay of Bengal.

After an uneventful passage the *Dunera* arrived in Madras at 0800 hours, 18th March. The Brigade disembarked during the forenoon and marched to a transit camp, where the Commandos would be billeted until continuing the journey onwards to Nasik.

7

India Once More

The city and port of Madras is situated on the Coromandel coast, the port facilities centred around an artificial harbour. Although first visited by Portuguese explorers, British pioneers established the first settlement around Fort St George in 1640. One hundred years later French troops overran the garrison, monopolising the region for the next 14 years. British troops drove the French out in 1760 and Madras remained part of British India until Indian Independence in 1947. The city's skyline is dominated by numerous towers and minarets. The 160 foot High Court Tower, as well as being ornamental also served as a lighthouse, its light being visible from a distance of 20 miles out at sea.

Shortly after the Brigade settled down in camp it became apparent that the messing facilities were very limited. To ease the problem meals were taken in relays, 44 drew the short straw and ate last. Almost as soon as the Brigade arrived in Madras the 'expatriates' kindly extended numerous social invitations to men of all ranks. Many of 44's marines took the opportunity to spend time with the British community in their homes.

The messing situation was resolved somewhat when all units were granted 14 days leave, commencing 26th March, the men of 3 Commando Brigade dispersing to all four corners of India. In the main 44's marines opted for either the big cities (Madras, Bangalore and Bombay), or the hill stations at Wellington and Ootacamund. Although only 350 miles from Madras, the hill stations offered a cool climate and a quiet, healthy environment.

The leave party bound for Bombay found reason to curse the Indian railway system when discovering that the Bombay express had departed 30 minutes earlier than scheduled. After much to-ing and fro-ing, 30 disgruntled bootnecks managed to hitch a ride on, ironically, the baggage train taking 44's stores and equipment to Nasik, via Bombay.

Almost as the last marine marched out of the camp to go on leave, the order was received for the unit to move on. With a large proportion of the Commando absent it fell to the small rear party to pack the unit's equipment for the transfer up to Nasik. Before leaving Madras three subalterns joined the Commando as replacement officers. The remaining personnel left the camp during the early evening 30th March, leaving Madras station on two trains for a routine night train journey through the Indian countryside.

Nasik
31st March–15th April 1945

Nasik, a place of great antiquity and sanctity, lies on the banks of the River Godavari, 107 miles to the north-east of Bombay. The legend of Rama, a classical Indian epic dating back to the 3rd Century BC can be identified with the town. Not unnaturally Nasik enjoys the prestige of being an important cultural centre of the Hindu faith; and as such was placed out of bounds to the soldiers and marines of the Commando Brigade.

When the Brigade arrived, the four Commandos were allocated adjoining tent lines and the advance parties were kept busy pitching tents and sorting stores. The delivery of an all new motor transport fleet: four 3-ton lorries, seven 15-cwt wagons, a jeep and eight motor cycles was the final cog in the wheel to put 44 back on a fully operational footing once more. The unit's strength was boosted when men wounded at Kangaw, including Lt O'Brien rejoined the Commando from hospital in Madras.

Somewhat strangely, and in direct contrast to its cultural and religious heritage, Nasik was also the home of a flourishing and renowned distillery. The officers' mess sergeant called at the distillery one morning to purchase several cases of assorted spirits. He was told that gin, brandy and rum were ready for collection, but could he please return in the afternoon for the whisky, as unfortunately, it was still too hot from the distilling process to bottle!

On 7th April prompt action by 'Royal' averted a potentially dangerous situation developing when fire broke out in the Quartermaster's stores. A strong wind fanned the blaze and several boxes of rifles and ammunition were manhandled away from the path of the flames before the fire was brought under control. With order restored the RSM began organising swimming parties, the bathers travelling 30 miles to Lake Beale to take the plunge.

The peace was shattered when Capt Watkins (A Tp) returned from a briefing at Brigade HQ with the news that 44's lines were to be given over to a Ghurka battalion of 25 Indian Infantry Division forthwith! The marines quickly moved in with 1 Commando and with all the hustle, bustle and a certain reluctance linked to such a measure it was not a good time to be in camp.

The military mind ordained that as soon as 44 had settled in with their comrades in 1, orders were issued for the Brigade to prepare to move 100 miles south to a camp in the Poona area. A Brigade advance party, including Capt Watkins and 25 marines from 44 left Nasik on 13th April. The men still on leave were directed by the appropriate authorities to rejoin the unit in Poona. During this period of organised chaos a reinforcing draft of four subalterns and ten marines joined the Commando.

Poona
16th April-4th May 1945

Poona was first mentioned in history in about 1604, notwithstanding that two of its Hindu temples date back to the 13th Century. After British forces defeated the indigenous Mahratta tribesmen in 1817/18, Poona was to become a major military headquarters and garrison. A large British Army presence was maintained in the area until Indian Independence. Lying 119 miles south-east of Bombay the town stands at a point where the rivers Mutha and Mula meet.

The first two days at Pashan Camp were extremely hectic for the advance party. The marines returning directly from leave to the new camp required blankets, mosquito nets, cutlery and all the usual stores; none of which had arrived from Nasik. However, by the time the main body of the Commando reached Pashan on 19th April everything was ship shape. Within hours of arriving, the commander of the newly formed 34 Indian Corps, Maj Gen O.L.Roberts CB, CBE, DSO paid the Brigade an informal visit.

During 44's sojourn in Poona the unit saw a change of commanding officer and several officers were transferred. On St Georges Day (23rd April) Lt Col Stockley was appointed to a position within Brigade HQ and command of the unit was made over to Lt Col D.B.Drysdale DSO, RM, previously the Brigade Major. The Commando also lost three more of its original officers: Capt E.M.Sturges was posted to HMS *Braganza* (Bombay); Lt A.R.White transferred back to the UK, sporting a black eye patch covering the wound received in Trincomalee. 'Gus' was probably the only serving Royal Marines officer to wear an eye patch at the time; Lt S.Henshall: appointed Brigade Demolitions Officer.

A practical joker 'par excellence' 44's late demolitions officer was held responsible for many mystery explosions. On one memorable occasion, the furniture in a makeshift officers mess was doctored. Any movement of selected chairs or tables triggered off small explosions in the adjacent jungle. One unsuspecting officer, 'spending a penny' amongst the jungle foliage was seriously inconvenienced when one of Sid Henshall's devices exploded alongside where the poor unfortunate was standing. The officer returned to the mess, his trousers in tatters vowing never to use the jungle for such purposes again. What he said to the demolitions officer is unprintable!

Lieutenants O'Brien, wounded on Pinner, and Powrie also returned to the UK at the same time. A reinforcing party of three officers and 30 marines joined the unit and Lt Brydon, wounded at Kangaw, was welcomed back to the Commando.

On 30th April, GOC 26 Indian Infantry Division, Maj Gen G.E.Lomax, called on the Brigade, inspecting 44's guard in the process. Shortly after the GOC's visit the Brigade was put on notice to move to Ahmadnagar, 72 miles to the north of its present location. Before leaving Pashan Camp, three separate events took place, all of which brought a mighty grin to the faces of 44's marines:

> a) the Sergeants' Mess held a dinner and dance, most of the female guests being nurses from the nearby hospitals;

> b) the Commando football team beat 42;

> c) several tents in both the officers and SNCOs lines, were knocked down during a heavy wind and rain storm. The monsoon season had almost arrived again!

On 1st May an advance party (Capts Hellis and Howarth, Lt Jack and 57 marines) left for Ahmadnagar, followed shortly after by the baggage party which travelled by road. The Commando left Pashan camp on 4th May, leaving at 0745 hours to board the special train that was to take the marines north. Not unusually the departure was delayed, the train finally leaving at 1000 hours. On arrival five hours later, the unit was transferred to the camp by motor transport.

Ahmadnagar/Londa
5th May-21st June 1945

Ahmadnagar, founded in 1490 was occupied in 1803 by British forces following a military siege. The besieging army was commanded by Sir Arthur Wellesley (later to become Duke of Wellington), in support of his brother, the Governor General (Richard Wellesley). The two brothers were instrumental in extending British influence, wiping out French power and curbing the authority of the native rulers. After its capture the city not only became an important garrison for the British

Army but also a significant mission centre. In 1901 the military fort, standing just to the east of the city was utilised to imprison Boer soldiers captured in South Africa during the Boer War.

Ahmadnagar was memorable for one special reason: whilst billeted there the Brigade learned that the war in Europe had ended. News of the German surrender was received on 8th May; 'Royal's' spontaneous initial reaction was to fire weapons skywards. Rifles, tommy guns, Verey pistols and 2' mortars (firing signal flares) were all discharged with gay abandon and with no thought of accounting for the ammunition used: the official celebrations were held on 9th May. The Commando assembled in the camp cinema to be addressed by the CO, a football match was hurriedly arranged between the SNCOs and JNCOs and every man received a free issue of one bottle of beer. In the field or forward camps, the official [free] issue of alcohol was limited to three, one pint bottles of Australian or Canadian beer per man, per month! Officers had the option of the same beer ration or a half bottle of spirits per month.

On 13th May 44 paraded, marching to church to attend a thanksgiving service for victory in Europe. The church parade was quickly followed by a 3 Commando Brigade ceremonial parade and march through the town; 44's X Tp representing the Commando.

The VE celebrations over, 44 was brought back down to earth with the news that the Commando was to tackle the jungle training course at Londa. The marines were left to speculate on where the next landings would take place! The climate was oppressively hot at Ahmadnagar at the time, being responsible for an unusually high number of prickly heat cases being seen by the doctor. All ranks were granted one day per week clear of all duties.

In the period before the unit moved south to Londa, the marines received the much coveted Garand rifles; plus the intensive training lectures associated with the issue of a new weapon. The Commando's structure was subjected to a minor reorganisation due to the disbandment of Y Tp. The displaced personnel: clerks, cooks, drivers, armourers etc. were absorbed into HQ Troop. At the same time, Capt Watkins was appointed adjutant, vice Capt Parish who took over Capt Watkin's former role as A Tp Leader.

An advance party of five officers and 26 marines (Capt Macan) set out for Londa on 15th May. No sooner had the detachment departed than Lt Col Drysdale received word that the move had been temporarily postponed. Mne R.Millar (A Tp) was not worried by the delay, his name had been drawn by the CO to take 28 days leave in the UK. On the eve of departure, the GOC 34 Indian Corps (Maj Gen O.L.Roberts) made an unannounced visit to the Commando. After turning out the guard he let it be known that he had been impressed by the marines' smartness and bearing.

The Commando began a tortuous journey to Londa on 21st May. The unit was moved by motor transport to the railway station, boarding the usual night train which pulled out at 2330 hours. The marines arrived in Poona at 0700 hours on 22nd May to spend the day either taking advantage of the swimming pool facilities put at their disposal or sight seeing. Food was provided by the Royal Army Catering Corps throughout the day as the Commandos whiled away the hours until the train resumed its journey at 0100 hours, 23rd May. Other than stopping at Koregaon for breakfast and Miraj for lunch, the train travelled virtually non-stop for 24 hours, reaching Londa at 0145, 24th May. The marines remained in their carriages until morning. At 0815 hours the Commando formed up to march off to their jungle quarters.

The Jungle Warfare School: Londa

The jungle warfare course was, for the majority, a chance to consolidate the lessons already learned in combat against the enemy. However the training schedule proved invaluable to the reinforcements who had joined the unit since 44 had returned from Kangaw. Some of the 'old Sweats' professed not to realize that they were even on a jungle training course, although they did reach the conclusion that 44 was being prepared for some future large scale operation. Ironically, before the Commando Depot at Achnacarry was established, each individual Commando unit had been charged with providing its own tutelage. 3 Commando Brigade had done likewise in regard to jungle training.

In general the ten day course encapsulated all that the marines had already experienced and learned from:

Jungle battle drills.

Field firing exercises: the riflemen using the recently issued Garand rifles for the first time on exercise.

Living off the jungle: improvising utensils for eating and drinking, identifying edible nuts, fruits and berries, lighting fires.

Night movement: marching between compass bearings, identifying jungle sounds.

Ambushes: setting up defensive boxes, sighting and digging weapon pits, making booby traps.

Signals exercises.

Sniper courses.

Attack/Defence competition.

The course was rounded off with a final exercise: a two day 'jolly' in thick jungle. The riflemen were impressed with the power of the Garand. A sub-section, firing in unison could destroy the side of a jungle hut using just one eight round clip of ammunition. Nature added the final touch of authenticity; heavy rain fell throughout the time 44 was in the jungle. Unlike Achnacarry, the course was completed without anyone in the Commando sustaining any serious injury. Recreation was confined to either swimming in a nearby river or a run ashore to Belgaum (between 1815 and 0030 hours).

The unit left Londa at 1800 hours, 4th June for an uneventful overnight journey back to Poona, arriving early in the afternoon, 5th June, two hours early. For those marines inclined, the next two hours were used to explore the historic town once more. The unit finally returned to Ahmadnagar in the late evening.

The remaining days at Ahmadnagar were dominated by the movement of personnel, the inter-troop field firing and efficiency competition, social events and football!

Another series of drafts resulted in five officers, ten NCO's and 46 marines being shifted to other units. Two lieutenants (Lts S.L.Fouche and D.Ranger) from the South African Union Defence Force and 13 marines joined 44 as replacement personnel.

The inter-troop competition was a keenly contested affair: the prize, a long weekend leave in Bombay. The syllabus, laid out in training memorandum No.13 contained the following disciplines:

Troop weapons:

Rifle: four groups, short advance and fire. Judged on: movement, fire control, accuracy. Marks: 200

Bren gun: As for rifle. Marks 200

Tommy gun: two pairs. Judged on: movement, accuracy of snap shooting. Marks: 40

Pistol: four men. As for Tommy gun. Marks: 40

Snipers: Two men, engage one target. Judged on: weapon handling, accuracy. Marks: 40

Grenade Launcher (M9A1): two teams per troop. Field firing: two targets, high and low angle. Judged on: movement, positioning, accuracy. Marks: 75

Grenade throwing: Six men. Each man throwing two x '36' and one x '77' grenades. Judged on: movement, positioning, accuracy. Marks: 75

2-inch Mortar: Two teams per troop. Field firing: high and low angle with high explosive smoke screen. Judged on: drill movement, fire control, accuracy. Marks: 100

Administration: Assessed when 'Duty Troop,' Hut inspection. Weapons inspection. Troop documentation and office procedure. Marks: 250

Parade work: For the last element of the competition, the Commando paraded in front of Brig Hardy at Kharakvasla, immaculately turned out in jungle 'greens,' white belts and anklets. The Brigadier conducted a thorough inspection of the marines on parade, taking a careful note of each troop's close order drill and finally took the salute as 44's marines marched past.

On the completion of the competition, A Tp were adjudged the winners.

The officers held a very successful dance in Ahmadnagar with invitations being extended to officers of neighbouring units. The local area commander, Maj Gen E.N.Goddard CBE, MVO, MC, attended the function, combining social and military duties; he formally inspected the Commando the next day. The junior NCOs opened their club; the CO congratulating the 'juniors' on the effort put into the venture. The new chaplain, Rev M.A.P.Wood, recently arrived from North-West Europe, invited men of all ranks to form a Commando choir. On 20th June an advance party (Lt Fouche) left for Kharakvasla, to be followed on 22nd June by the main body. The unit was transported to the new camp in a convoy of 27 Royal Indian Army Service Corps 3-ton trucks.

Kharakvasla
22nd June-17th August 1945

The move to the Combined Operations Training Centre No. 3 at Kharakvasla, a town lying to the south-west of Poona and close to Lake Fife was the fifth change of camp since the Brigade had arrived at

Nasik 12 weeks earlier. On arrival the marines of *44* found their camp lines still occupied by marines of 34 Amphibious Support Regiment. The Commandos were assigned temporary billets until alternative quarters could be found and for once *44* was to profit from an initial setback. When permanent accommodation was finally arranged, the Commando was to be the only unit in the Brigade allocated huts: the monsoon broke shortly after 'Royal' settled in!

The last week in June was spent perfecting both parade marching and close order drill in readiness for the Brigade Commander's inspection. The unit forfeited the services of yet another of the former 3RM officers when Capt Parish was transferred out of the Commando. Major P.Wood was drafted to *44* as 2i/c and Lts J.A.Smith and J.I.H.Owen were promoted to captain. In the subsequent reshuffle Capt Smith replaced Capt Parish as A Tp leader and Capt Owen took over S Tp. On 30th June the Brigadier took the salute at the all important Commando parade with 42's pipe band providing music to march by. Brig Hardy was later to send a message of congratulations to the CO, commenting on the very smart turn out and precision displayed by *44*.

Lt Col Drysdale and officers, Kharakvasla, July 1945

July 1945

As the pace of training was stepped up, it became obvious that the Brigade had been earmarked for a large-scale amphibious operation somewhere. Lt Col Drysdale and the RSM preached the virtues of strong leadership, properly co-ordinated section tactics and fire control at a series of lectures given to all NCO's. The Commando carried out field firing and signals exercises, opposed assault landings and cross country marches. Every marine in the unit attended an intensive close-quarter combat course under Capt Owen.

During the course of training, the Achnacarry curse struck again. Three marines of B Tp were wounded by 2-inch mortar splinters. All three men were hospitalised.

Lt Gen Christison spent a day with the Commando to monitor the training programme. After lunching with the officers the general watched a demonstration of village clearance techniques carried out by C Tp.

Towards the end of July a detachment from the Royal Artillery (three officers and 26 other ranks) were temporarily attached, the gunners' role being to support the Brigade during a large-scale amphibious landing exercise planned for early August. Time off was limited, but the marines had time to have a run ashore in Poona, attend resettlement courses given by Maj M.H.Davies (42 RM Commando) or watch the Brigade football team in action.

The Commando lost another stalwart from 3RM days when Capt O.St.J.Hamlin MBE, together with four other officers moved on to pastures new. The Commando's strength was boosted by a replacement draft of 38 marines.

August 1945

The planned invasion of Malaya (Operation Zipper) by the recently formed 34 Indian Corps was scheduled to be launched on 9th September. The Commando Brigade would lead the assault on Port Dickson by 23 Indian Infantry Division (less one Brigade) on D+3 (12th September). The commandos would be put ashore, charged with the task of seizing the town and dock area before nightfall. The landing and advance would be made across flat open beaches. Intelligence information in regard to enemy defences was sketchy, although it was known that all the jetties in the dock area were protected by fortified machine gun positions.

It was safe to assume that the open beaches were covered by machine guns, mortars and artillery. It was expected that the Commando Brigade would incur heavy casualties before their mission was completed.

On 5th August 44 took part in an amphibious landing exercise code-named 'Lilliput.' It became very clear that this was a rehearsal for the invasion of Malaya. The Commando was brought up to strength when an additional draft of 50 marines arrived in the days leading up to 'Lilliput.' On the eve of the exercise the CO addressed the Commando gathered in the camp cinema to outline 44's role in the exercise. On 5th August reveille was sounded at 0515 hours after which the marines were organised to form up by boatload before marching to the assembly point. The Commando landed at 0830 hours and by lunch time all its designated tasks had been completed. To round off a nice morning out 'Royal' returned to camp in motor transport.

Commandos of 44 wearing US pattern steel helmets whilst training for Operation Zipper. The Commando Brigade opted for the green beret, despite Lady Mountbatten's concern over the number of headwounds suffered by the Commandos.

6th August:

Whilst 44 staged one of its celebrated concerts for the Brigade in the camp cinema, an American B29 Superfortress 'Enola Gay' dropped the first atomic bomb (9,000lbs and 10 feet long, code named 'Little Boy') on Hiroshima. As the unit returned to business, practising assault landings and night exercises during which Lt Fouche (A Tp) was wounded by grenade shrapnel; yet more atomic devastation was about to fall on mainland Japan.

9th August:

A second slightly larger atomic bomb (10,000lbs, 10 feet long and code named 'Fat man') was dropped on Nagasaki. The destructive power of each bomb was estimated to be equal to 20,000 tons of high explosive. Although at the time no one was aware that the Second World War was nearly over, news that Russia had entered the war against Japan by invading Manchuria was welcomed by all and sundry.

10th August:

Unaware that two atomic bombs had been dropped, the Commandos were more than a little surprised, when, during the day news was received that Japan had began the process of negotiating peace terms.

11th August:

The day was spent hastily packing stores and equipment in preparation for a short notice move that was 'on the cards' in the wake of the momentous air raids launched on 6th and 9th August.

12th August:

Lt Col Drysdale attended a conference at Brigade HQ and on his return spoke to the unit mustered in the cinema. 44 had to be packed and ready to move by 2000 hours; it was envisaged that the Commando would be leaving sometime the next morning. The destination was unclear but there was a very strong possibility that the marines would be involved in garrison duties. The unit was then caught by the 'hurry up and wait' syndrome; the intended move was postponed later in the evening.

13th August:

The Commando's planned departure was on/off several times throughout the day. As the unit waited for orders, 'Royal' was totally unimpressed with the monsoon weather which the marines knew would severely hinder any movement by road.

14th August:

Started off as a re-run of the previous day, until the Commando was ordered to stand by for an urgent move to an undisclosed destination, leaving at 0600 hours, 15th August, and the CO received a very urgent call to attend a hurriedly convened conference at Brigade HQ.

15th August:

Emperor Hirohito made a nationwide radio broadcast to his people, informing them of his government's decision to surrender to the Allies. When the news reached 44, the marines were not surprised that the 'urgent move' was postponed. In direct contrast to VE day, the Japanese capitulation was greeted with some caution. As enthusiastic crowds gathered in front of Buckingham Palace and revelled in London's Trafalgar Square and Piccadilly Circus to celebrate the final end of WW2, 44's thoughts were still firmly focused on the planned assault against the enemy in Malaya. The question asked, would the infamous Japanese soldier believe and accept the terms of surrender?

16th August:

A thanksgiving service for victory over Japan was held in the canteen at 0930 hours. Later in the morning, a small advance party left by road to travel direct to Bombay. In the meantime 44 boarded motor transport for the journey into Poona, the marines destined to take one last journey, compliments of the Indian railway system, to Bombay. Before the train left Poona at 0520 hours (17th August) the results of a certain amount of high jinks were laid at the door of 44. Tonga (rickshaw) ponies and government owned bullocks were found mysteriously wandering the streets unattended. Victory flags hanging from public buildings and 'pukka' clubs mysteriously disappeared and general high spirits prevailed. The flags were later to be seen draped from every carriage window as the train pulled away from Poona station.

17th August:

The train arrived in Bombay at 1245 hours and the marines marched from the railway station to the docks. On arrival at the jetty the Commando embarked onto the Infantry Landing Ship HMS *Glengyle* in company with their usual travelling companions, 5 Commando.

Seatime V
Bombay to Hong Kong
18th August-11th September 1945

HMS *Glengyle* was one of three sister ships (*Glenearn* and *Glenroy*) taken over by the Admiralty on completion of building in 1939. The 13,000 ton, twin screw motor ships, had a service speed of 18 knots. Designed for the Far Eastern trade, the three vessels were being built for Alfred Holt's Glen Line. The *Glengyle* was immediately adapted to carry landing craft: 24 LCA's and three LCM's all hoisted on davits, with 12 Bren gun carriers stowed on deck.

Accommodation was provided for 78 officers and 630 troops, eight officers and 122 men (landing craft crews), 37 officers and 218 ratings (ship's company).

The ship's galley could comfortably cater for over 1100 men. The armament for anti-aircraft defence consisted of six 4-inch high angle guns, four two-pdr pom-poms and seven Oerlikon guns on single mountings.

Before reaching the Far East, HMS *Glengyle* had seen extensive service in the Mediterranean, being involved in the major landings at Anzio, Sicily and Syria; Operation Torch (North Africa) and the ill-fated Dieppe raid. The vessel was returned to the Merchant Service (Glen Line) in 1948.

The *Glengyle* set sail in convoy at 0800 hours, 18th August, immediately running into a heavy sea swell; many men tasted breakfast again! Although the Brigade's destination was still thought to be Malaya (Penang Island), rumours were rife that the ships would be diverted elsewhere. On 22nd August the uncertainty of current events was emphasized when the convoy unexpectedly steamed into Trincomalee and dropped anchor in the outer harbour. The Commandos stayed on board in 'Trinco' for nine days whilst the Brigade's future role was being determined.

The time was spent undertaking activities both military and social. The two embarked Commandos provided the necessary manpower for 'Puddleduck,' a training exercise designed to test the landing craft crews' proficiency in loading and landing troops. Brigadier Hardy with his staff moved over to *Glengyle*, staying on board for several days before transferring to HMCS *Ontario* for the onward passage. On 28th August, Major General Wildman-Lushington (GOC Commando Group) visited the ship. After lunch the General addressed the assembled officers and SNCOs of 5 and 44 telling them of the Brigade's revised destination: Hong Kong.

Another day, another general; on 29th August the military force commander, Major General F.W.Festing CB, CBE, DSO (GOC Land Forces, Hong Kong) arrived on board *Glengyle* to hold conferences with the Brigade's senior officers and others. Now that 44's destination and probable duties had been determined, the entire Commando was quickly landed to enable 44's marines to brush up their close order drill. The unit utilised the local football field as a parade ground and the men drilled under the eagle eye of the Regimental Sergeant Major.

When the men were not involved in things military, they were allowed limited periods of shore leave. Most headed for either the Fleet Canteen to cash in the beer tickets issued on board the *Glengyle* or went to one of Trincomalee's numerous unspoilt beaches. A team regatta, held alongside the ship was won by 44's officers, much to the chagrin of the other entrants. On board the ship, an open air showing of the film 'Mask of Dimitrious' was brought to an abrupt end when a rainstorm of monsoon proportions suddenly developed. Before the convoy left Trincomalee so did a number of men in Age and Service group 26. With the war over, demobilisation was on the horizon for the 'Hostilities Only' men.

On 31st August, following an abnormal amount of nautical manoeuvring outside the harbour, the *Glengyle* joined HMCS *Ontario* and HMIS *Llanstephan Castle* to continue the voyage eastwards towards Hong Kong. Once at sea Lt Col Drysdale spoke to each troop individually. The CO outlined the scope of operations to be undertaken by 44 when they reached Hong Kong. He expressed the view that the Commando Brigade would undoubtedly receive a warm and friendly welcome from the population at large. The unit could expect to work at full stretch for approximately one month before being relieved by other troops: that part of the operation definitely did not happen as planned! The convoy was scheduled to reach Singapore five days after leaving 'Trinco.' The vessels carrying the Brigade would have the dubious honour of being in the midst of the first Allied convoy to sail through the Straits of Malacca; the narrow expanse of sea which separates the Malay peninsular from the island of Sumatra. The Japanese navy had laid numerous minefields in this stretch of water and the likelihood of uncharted sea mines floating into the path of the ships was a real and frightening possibility.

On 5th September the convoy was joined by two tank landing craft carrying the Brigade's vehicles. As the ships approached the recognised area of dangerous waters, speed was reduced, extra look-outs were posted, the lower decks were cleared and all hatches were battened down. At daybreak 6th September, the *Glengyle* was joined by a host of additional warships and transports. Aircraft carriers, cruisers, destroyers and merchant ships swelled the size of the convoy for the passage through the Straits. By mid-morning several vessels had dropped astern of the main mass of ships, heading for destinations unknown. The ships carrying the Brigade were accompanied by HM Cruisers *Ontario* and *Cleopatra*, three destroyers, an escort carrier and a merchantman. The ships formed up in 'single line ahead' to pass within three miles of the entrance to Singapore harbour. HMS *Cleopatra* detached to enter the port, followed later in the afternoon by the three destroyers.

The main occupation on the remaining three days of the voyage was to conserve the fresh water supply which was beginning to run dangerously low. The men on board received inoculations against cholera and lectures on the treatment of Japanese prisoners of war and other captured personnel. As always 5 and 44 travelled well together and before the ship reached its destination the two units staged the usual concert parties on the upper deck. Immediately prior to the convoy reaching Hong Kong all embarked troops were issued with 48 hour ration packs.

8
Hong Kong 1945-1947

The British Crown Colony of Hong Kong was to be 44's home until the unit was renumbered as 40(RM) Commando in March 1947, prior to the Commando Brigade's relocation to Malta. The Colony consists of Hong Kong, an island eleven miles long and between two and five miles wide, situated at the mouth of the Pearl River; Kowloon, a peninisular on the Chinese mainland; The New Territories, the borderlands between the Colony and Nationalist China. The Colony has a total land area of approximately 400 square miles.

British forces secured the Island of Hong Kong when fighting the first Opium War (1839-42). During the Battle of San-Yuan-Li, a detachment of Royal Marines successfully rescued a company of three British officers and 60 Indian sepoys, cut off and surrounded by a large force of Chinese irregular soldiers outside the city of Canton. The Kowloon Peninsular was ceded from China in 1860 following the second Opium War, with the New Territories being leased (99 years) from the Chinese Government in 1898. The whole region became a major outpost of Britain's Far Eastern defence network. During the Second World War, the Japanese army overran the Colony in Christmas week 1941. Hong Kong island was captured on Christmas Day. The Commando Brigade furnished the main element of the British land forces sent to reoccupy, administer and police the Colony following the Japanese surrender.

At one time it was by no means certain that the Colony would be returned to British rule at the end of hostilities in the Far East. Nationalist China saw an opportunity to regain sovereignty of the territory; a reward for the nation's war effort against Japan. As early as 1942 US President Roosevelt became committed to China's cause; America willing to see the United Kingdom's influence in the area diminished. The Sino-American stand against British interests induced a great deal of political in-fighting between the three governments.

The newly elected Labour Government of 1945 under Mr Attlee was adamant that the colony would remain under British control. The Prime Minister affirmed that the colony would only be returned to China as part of a general settlement in Asia; including Holland giving up the Dutch East Indies and the USA forgoing their interests in Hawaii. In the absence of such an agreement Hong Kong would remain part of the British Empire. The diplomatic position between the UK and China in respect of Hong Kong was so muddled that the Japanese generals were

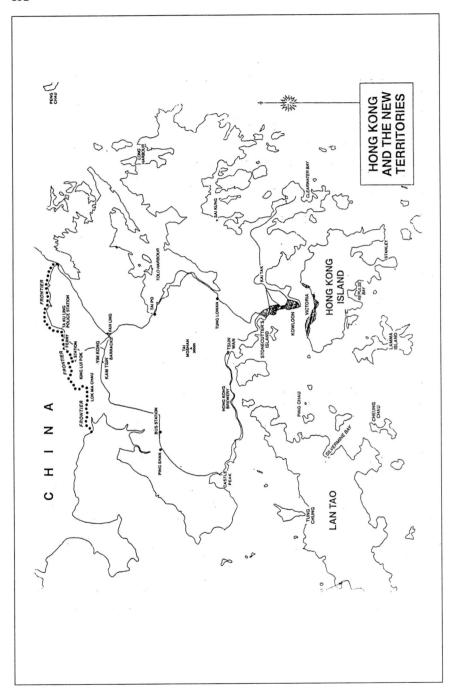

uncertain who would receive their surrender! On the death of President Roosevelt America's attitude softened, President Truman directed General Douglas McArthur to arrange for British commanders to accept the surrender of Hong Kong. The Chinese were unhappy to be sidelined in such a way and the Nationalist Chinese Army's resentment was to become very apparent to the Brigade in future months.

When the Commando Brigade arrived, the region was in a state of complete shambles. The harbour was littered with wrecked ships. Tugs and other small craft were found sunk alongside piers and only three wharves were usable. Not one single dock-side crane was in working order. The chaos created a major supply problem for the authorities, the citizens of Hong Kong already suffering the effects of a rice famine. It was estimated that a supply of 25,000 tons of rice per month would be required to feed the 700,000 people in the Colony. All staple foodstuffs, rice, flour and sugar were put on ration. Fortunately all the water supply pipelines had been maintained in good working order. The electricity supply could not be guaranteed due to damage to the generating plant and lack of fuel - there was a serious shortage of timber and coal. Domestic gas production, the telephone system and public transport were almost non-existent. The prevailing conditions led to a certain amount of labour unrest among workers, wages could not keep up with the rampant inflation of prices. The situation was exacerbated further by the blanket refusal of the Chinese Nationalist government to impose immigration controls. Chinese people flooded into Hong Kong.

From the arrival of British Naval forces (Rear Admiral R.A.Harcourt CB, CBE) in August until the end of 1945, over 400,000 people crossed over the border from China into the Colony. A military administration (Admiral Harcourt was appointed C-in-C, Hong Kong) was established by proclamation on 1st September. The colony remained under military control until civil government was restored on 1st May 1946.

The *Glengyle* arrived in Hong Kong at 0900 hours, 11th September and anchored near the British battleship HMS *Anson*. Lt Col Drysdale was immediately called to attend a conference on board HMCS *Ontario*; the Commando remaining on board for the remainder of the day. 44 disembarked in the early afternoon on the next day, 12th September, and was billeted on the mainland in quarters in and around Kowloon's Peninsula Hotel. The remainder of the day was spent transferring stores and equipment ashore; the task being completed before the start of the strict curfew imposed at 2200 hours. When the Commando went on parade the next morning, the marines were told the type of duties which the unit would undertake. At the time there were literally thousands of Japanese military personnel in the colony awaiting repatriation. During the next few days streets were cleared and sanitation arrangements improved; 100 Japanese prisoners of war being utilized to provide a labour force. When time permitted, organised parties were taken on guided tours to see at first-hand the consequences of the Japanese occupation.

On 16th September the Commando moved into the northern area of Kowloon. POW working parties were used to clear the accommodation areas before 'Royal' set up home. At 1600 hours HMS *Anson* fired a 21 gun salute to mark the time of the official Japanese surrender of the colony. On the following day A Tp with 42's pipe band in support provided a guard of honour for Maj Gen Festing's arrival on the mainland when he came ashore at Kowloon Jetty. When all the ceremonial duties honouring the official surrender were concluded 44 got down to business. The Commando turned out armed patrols to protect the unit's area of operations from looters, armed robbers and other criminal elements at large in the town. Hotels and houses were raided in the search for illegally held weapons and numerous looters and armed civilians were arrested.

Whitfield Barracks, used to house Japanese civilian internees, was raided by a combined detachment from A, X, and S Tps, plus 42's B Tp. The marines found caches of weapons, ammunition and large sums of money hidden away during the detailed search of the barracks. Other tasks performed by 'Royal' included controlling the volatile rice queues, general policing and military security duties. One gang of criminals always appeared dressed in black silk pyjama suits and were particularly active in the Mong Kok area of the town. This band of brigands carried out three armed robberies on two successive days without being apprehended.

The Commando's sentries had to be especially vigilant to keep looters and other undesirables away from the unit's accommodation, offices and stores. On more than one occasion marines guarding 44's base area returned the fire of groups of armed men bent on committing illegal acts.

On 25th September 44 received a visit from a group of VIPs in numbers never before encountered. Headed by the Secretary of State (War), the Rt Hon. J.J.Lawson MP, his entourage included Rear Admiral C.J.Harcourt, CB, CBE (C-in-C Hong Kong), Major General F.W.Festing CB, CBE, DSO (GOC Land Forces, Hong Kong), Captain J.A.S.Eccles CBE, RN, Group Captain Barker RAF, Brigadier C.R.Hardy DSO, RM, the Chief of Police and other officers. The Guard of Honour was found by B Tp with 42's pipe band supplying the music. The Secretary of State took the salute as the marines marched past the saluting dais outside the Peninsula Hotel. The marines' endeavour was rewarded with an issue of rum on return to quarters.

At the end of the month 44's marines undertook the formidable task of searching and completing the documentation of 600 Formosan nationals being transferred into the Whitfield Barracks Internment Camp.

Marines of A Tp at Pui Ching School, Kowloon 1945 (top); and 25 years on... (Maj Gen J.I.H.Owen on left in bottom picture).

October 1945

Following a full dress rehearsal, two separate victory parades were held on 9th October in Kowloon and on Hong Kong island. The Brigade Commander, Brig Hardy took the salute as 44 marched past the Peninsula Hotel in Kowloon, whilst 20 marines drawn from the rifle troops (Maj J.A.Gilks) went across to the island to represent the unit at the Commander-in-Chief's parade.

Both mobile and foot patrols were kept busy apprehending looters, robbers and other criminals. The bootnecks also controlled civil unrest, sought-out Chinese guerrillas and Nationalist Army deserters. The Commando's quartermaster's store was broken into, the thieves escaping with 140 pairs of green battledress trousers and 25 blouses. With life in the Colony slowly returning to pre-war standards the attempted theft of the cricket nets from the local club was almost catastrophic. Fortunately one of 44's patrols caught four Chinese youths red handed as they tried to escape.

A, C and S Tps assumed the role of prison officers when they were required to escort large numbers of Japanese civilian internees from Whitfield Barracks across to Stanley prison camp on Hong Kong island. The Commando put a strong detachment of men into the centre of Kowloon on 10th October to police the Chinese National Day celebrations.

The demobilisation of 'Hostilities Only' ranks began to gain momentum with the release of men for discharge; it being obvious that the vast majority of 44's marines would be leaving the unit in the coming months. The imminent parting of so many close comrades motivated the CO, together with representatives from all elements of the unit, to form the 44 (RM) Commando Old Comrades Association. The inaugural meeting took place on 8th October. The plans were well laid as a reunion of the Commando has been held in London every year from 1946 up to the present time. The HOs were not the only men returning to the United Kingdom, Brig C.R.Hardy DSO,** relinquished command of the Brigade to return home. Before leaving, the Brigade Commander addressed the unit; once again passing on his personal congratulations in respect of the unit's efficiency and performance during all the Arakan battles and subsequent operations.

As the immediate post-war tensions started to ease so the unit's social life picked up. The talented 44 concert party attained an even wider audience when they gave a 35 minute broadcast over Radio Station 2BW Hong Kong on Chinese National Day. The Commando entertainers also put on the cabaret show at a dance held by HQ Tp.

November 1945

The month was dominated by visits from senior officers and a change of command, both of the Brigade and 44. Elements of the unit were redeployed and the movement of personnel continued.

The GOC Land Forces was becoming a regular visitor to the unit. On 1st November Maj Gen Festing watched a charity football match when 44 played a Chinese XI, the marines winning 6-0; 42's pipe band entertaining the crowd during the half-time interval. All the proceeds of the event were donated to the Fund for the Relief of the Distressed in China. Maj Gen Festing's second visit was to conduct a formal inspection of the Commando. On 16th November the unit paraded in honour of the Chief of the Imperial General Staff, Field Marshal Lord Alanbrooke. The Guard of Honour was found from X Tp. Three days later the new Brigade Commander, Brigadier H.D.Fellowes, DSO, RM (42's ex-commanding officer) also carried out a formal inspection of the Commando. B Tp provided the Guard of Honour.

The changes at the top were completed when 44's CO, Lt.Col D.B.Drysdale relinquished his command before flying back to England to take up a staff appointment. The 2i/c, Major N.P.Wood MC, assumed command of the unit on his promotion to lieutenant colonel. Major General Festing called on 44 for a third time in November, on this occasion paying a courtesy call on the new CO.

The Commando provided two separate 30 man detachments (Capt D.F.Furlong and Lt J.C.Grey) to escort POWs being repatriated back to Japan from Hong Kong. For the marines involved the detached duty made a welcome change from the incessant patrolling and security raids being carried out in Kowloon. As the crime wave receded 44 began to spread out to patrol and police a wider area. A Tp were the first marines to move, being deployed to cover an island lying to the west of Hong Kong called Lan Tao. Before 'Royal' moved across to Lan Tao in LCA's, the CO and 2i/c had already carried out an initial 'recce' of the island. On the return trip Lt Col Wood received a slight injury from flying debris when a small explosion occured on the launch carrying the two officers back to Kowloon.

The Commando was beginning a period of transformation, as men left 44 for 'de-mob,' they were being replaced by marines fresh out of training. The time had come to re-mould the unit. After five years of hard training and fighting, the unit had achieved an excellent standard of military skills, bearing and discipline. The marines who had been with the Commando since the unit was first formed as 3rd Battalion Royal Marines, had experienced most of the ups and downs of service life, including warfare at its most brutal. The replacement drafts of men quite naturally had no unit spirit and some, after spending a prolonged period in the Holding Commando had lost some of the 'snap' vital to any proud company of men. It was important for the 'old soldiers' to encourage the replacements to attain and maintain the current high standards required of all 44's marines. Past experience had proved that good discipline was based on mutual respect, good administration and high morale. The outward and visible signs were keen eyed alertness, smart saluting, an immaculate turn-out and responsible behaviour on leave. 44 was an excellent example of the Royal Marines' unparalleled reputation for producing units of the finest quality.

December 1945

The Commando Brigade's ability to carry out all the tasks assigned to it was becoming seriously open to doubt due to the ever-increasing manpower deficiencies. Even though the Royal Navy provided 1700 sailors for shore patrols and the Royal Air Force contributed 1000 airmen for security duties, the Commando Brigade assumed the lion's share of all internal security responsibilities. The three armed services were required to provide the necessary resources to:

- undertake the duties of a 2800 man civilian police force.

- provide guards for VIPs, food stores, public buildings.

- man the border posts and maintain frontier patrols.

- set up and man security posts in outlying villages.

- act as guardians over 22,000 Japanese POW's and civilian internees.

- mount mobile patrols to round up armed bands of guerrillas, communist infiltrators, looters and pirates.

In addition to the duties listed above, movements staff were required to facilitate the smooth passage of the Chinese 8th and 13th Armies passing through British territory to embark on ships moored alongside Kowloon's dock piers.

The shortage of manpower was creating a crisis of such magnitude that the C-in-C Hong Kong was forced to send a signal to the Combined Chiefs of Staff in London requesting that more troops be sent to booster the Colony's Garrison. Rear Admiral Harcourt's concern was that the intended release of the next batch of men for discharge would reduce the Brigade's strength to such an extent that the

Commandos would not be in a position to meet their commitments. The point was well made that if an additional Brigade was not sent to reinforce Hong Kong's Land Forces, the C-in-C would be compelled to retain the services of the next batch of men awaiting discharge.

The C-in-C's signal concentrated the minds of those involved admirably. The Combined Chiefs' response was threefold:

1. Admiral Harcourt was directed to release the men for discharge as planned.

2. The Supreme Allied Commander, SEAC, was directed to transfer 150 Indian Infantry Brigade to Hong Kong forthwith.

3. The C-in-C was told to expect a further 800 Royal Marine Commandos in January, 1946. This number would include one complete Commando (45 RM), reinforcements for 42 and 44 plus men from the Commando Holding Centre at Lake Beale (Ahmadnager) which had been earmarked for immediate closure.

Due to political upheavals in India and Malaya, Lord Louis Mountbatten had, up to now, been juggling the land forces under his command to cover all eventualities. The political uncertainties in India required that British rather than Indian troops be retained on the sub-continent. At the same time C-in-C Hong Kong would have preferred additional British troops be sent to the colony to guard the frontier and deal with the thousands of Nationalist troops passing through the New Territories to reach Kowloon's docks.

Admiral Harcourt's hopes were dashed when 6 Brigade, 2nd British Infantry Division, already nominated to move to Hong Kong were diverted to Malaya to reinforce that area of political unrest. The 150 Indian Brigade, being the only formation ready to undertake a rapid redeployment were moved to the Colony. The advance party arrived on the 19th December, being followed by the remainder of the Indian Brigade on the 30th December.

The Commando Brigade's recognised establishment had always been four Commando units, therefore the two Army Commandos (1 and 5), whose ranks had been reduced by the release of men for discharge would amalgamate to become 1/5 Army Commando. With the impending arrival of 45, the Brigade would have 1/5 Army and 42, 44, 45(RM) Commandos under its command.

44, unaware of the politics of the situation, were spreading their troops further afield. With A Tp already ensconced on Lan Tao island, B Tp (Ping Shan) and X Tp (Tsun Wan) moved up into the New Territories. C Tp relieved men of 1 Commando on Cheung Chau and Ping Chau islands, with S and HQ Tps the only marines of of the unit remaining in Kowloon. The Commando was spread far and wide. Later in the month all five troops were rotated between the six locations occupied by 44's marines.

With 'Royal' policing some of the Colony's offshore islands the Commando reverted back to the 'Per Mare' function, namely anti-piracy patrols. Six motor launches were provided for the Commando Brigade's use. Ideally four craft would be patrolling the waters around Hong Kong and the neighbouring islands at any one time. A motorised skiff was used to operate between Tai O and Cheung Chau. The crews of the patrol worked under the direct orders of the Superintendent of the Water Police, Colonel Pittendrigh. Their duties included:

> - Paying regular weekly visits to the outlying islands and riverside villages.

> - Gathering information concerning illegal waterborne activities.

> - Inspecting firearms licences issued by the Hong Kong authorities.

> - Examining junk licences. All Chinese junks required licences to trade or fish in British waters. An exception was made for vessels sheltering from bad weather.

For the marines not involved with the anti-piracy operations, shoreside patrolling was increased. The foot patrols were replaced with mobile units consisting of one officer/SNCO, five marines plus a Chinese interpreter. The unit's strength was boosted by the return of Capt Furlong and his detachment from Japan and the arrival of Maj C.L.Price RM (2i/c) and Lt M.T.Denham.

As 44 was spread between six separate troop locations, unit social activities were virtually non-existent; although a small ENSA party did entertain B and X Tps at the beginning of the month. 'Royal' celebrated Christmas at the individual troop locations. The GOC (Maj Gen Festing) accompanied by Brig Fellowes and the CO visited B, C and X Tps on Christmas day. 1945 was for many, the last Christmas spent in the service. 1946 was to see the vast majority of 44's 'old sweats' returning home to pick up the threads of civilian life once more.

1946:

As the world slowly became accustomed to peace so Britain's armed forces were drastically reduced; the Services returning to peacetime strengths and organisation. The Ministry of Labour and National Service had been pre-planning for the mass demobilisation of the country's servicemen and women since before the Second Front was opened on the continent of Europe. A joint working party of politicians, civil servants and officers from the three Services created a system of demobilisation that was to work surprisingly well. A simple formula was produced based on two elements, a) year of birth, and b) the year of joining the service (sub-divided into quarters). The two elements were transposed to form a graph; where the two variables met produced a 'group number.' The lowest group numbers represented the oldest men with the longest service, demobilisation being based on the release of men and women in the lowest groups first. Men aged 50 and over were given an overriding priority for discharge. The formula also included a another detail; Class A and B release. Class A: men in general employment. Class B: tradesmen in occupations essential to the post-war rebuilding programme. The scheme was designed to provide early discharge to men and women previously employed in certain occupations and whose expertise was vital for the major reconstruction work necessary for the revitalisation of Britain's economy. i.e, the building industry, mining and education. Class B was a minefield to those responsible for granting early release for discharge. Many men in all three services declared themselves to be pre-war bricklayers, plumbers, electricians etc. in an attempt to gain early release. One exception made to the rules governing Class B release concerned the Police Service. The Metropolitan Police for example had engaged 4000 women, 3000 'time expired' officers and 15,000 police war reserves out of a total force of 62,800. In early 1946, early discharge was granted to men wishing to enter the police service on release from the forces.

The intention of government planning was to release 750,000 men and women from all three services by the end of 1945. In reality the numbers released for discharge reached one million by the end of that year. The Cabinet was keen to accelerate the procedure to secure the release of a further three million service personnel by June 1946.

For 44 the turnover of personnel was almost 100% by the end of 1946. After a slow start the demob process quickened dramatically. The first men left the unit in September 1945 (Age and Service Group 26) and by March 1946, men in groups up to No. 47 had been released. Later in the year, men who had completed two years service were beginning to be released. The unit's establishment was maintained by the a steady flow of national service marines. The replacement drafts in January, July, September, October and November numbered around 50 per month. Drafts of 90 plus in March and May replaced the large batch of men discharged in Age and Service Groups 32-47.

January:

The Commando remained scattered during the early months of the year. The unit held a Remembrance Service, conducted by the Rev Wood on 24th January for those men of the Commando who lost had their lives defending 'Pinner' one year previously.

On 29th January Col C.F.Phillips DSO, RM (Fleet Royal Marine Officer) British Pacific Fleet came ashore to inspect the Commando.

31st January was designated 'Kangaw Day,' all members of the Brigade being granted one day's holiday to coincide with the end of the Commando's involvement with the Kangaw operation. On the same day the CO Lt Col Wood attended 5 Commando's remembrance service held to honour the soldiers and marines of all four units who lost their lives defending Hill 170 over the 12 day period of operations.

February:

The 1st February signalled the start of the Chinese New Year. A composite detachment drawn from A, S, and HQ Tps was placed on immediate standby to quell any disturbances in the town.

On 4th February Lord Louis Mountbatten paid his third visit to the Brigade since the Commandos had come under his command. After inspecting the parade the Supreme Allied Commander, SEAC, passed on his congratulations to the assembled units of the Brigade, talking of the vital role that the Brigade had played in the Burma Campaign. Lord Louis had personally selected 3 Commando Brigade for, in his words, 'one of the most important tasks of the post war, the re-occupation of Hong Kong.' Lord Mountbatten's admiration of Commando Forces was well known to the Brigade. In a personal letter to General Sir Claude Auchinleck (C-in-C, India) he wrote 'As you know, I take a great personal interest in these troops, since they were very much my concern as Chief of Combined Operations and ever since I have constituted myself a guardian of their interests as far as I am able to help them.' Later in the day Lord Louis travelled up to the New Territories to visit C Tp ensconced at Castle Peak.

One week later Lt Col Wood, relinquished command of 44 (11th February). The 2i/c Major Price was promoted to lieutenant colonel and assumed command.

The GOC (Gen Festing) kept tabs on the unit by visiting individual troops at their locations at Tung Chung and on the islands of Lan Tao, Cheung Chau and Ping Chau.

March to May:

The Commando moved up to Fan Ling (New Territories) to relieve 1/5 Commando on 4th March. A and HQ Tps settled into the barracks whilst the remainder of the unit were billeted in and around Lena Lodge. Although six months had elapsed since the reoccupation of the colony, the border areas still posed a problem for the security forces. Patrol duties included:

- monitoring the food situation.

- explaining the new currency notes in circulation and the associated financial legislation.

- enforcing the Arms regulations and accepting surrendered weapons.

- being alert to the possibility of renegade Japanese soldiers being at large in the region.

- last but by no means least 'Royal' was to 'show the flag.' The Chinese Nationalist Army (CNA), still hostile to Britain's retention of the Colony instituted a phase of intense sabre rattling while 44 guarded the frontier between the colony and China. In April a series of incidents heightened tensions between the CNA and 44's marines.

During the period 13th-15th April, the friction between the two became acute; CNA troops opened fire on an anti-smuggling patrol as the marines confiscated illicit stocks of flour discovered in a border village. As the Chinese troops were at extreme range, fire was not returned. A group of CNA soldiers threatened another of 44's anti-smuggling patrols with iron bars and in a third incident a patrol returned fire when coming under attack from a section of CNA troops. Two Chinese soldiers were hit in the exchange; one of the wounded men was treated by 44's medics in the unit aid post.

The sensitive situation was defused following a joint visit to the area by Maj Gen Festing and Maj Gen Kwok (CNA). General Festing was adroit in his dealings with the Chinese Nationalist military authorities. His close contact and cordial relationship with his CNA opposite number was primarily responsible for the avoidance of a serious escalation of incidents involving Chinese troops. Although conditions improved somewhat, a directive was issued to the Commando; 'all ranks were to carry arms at all times when away from the barracks or troop billets.'

The situation remained relatively calm for a period of three weeks. In early May matters erupted once more: an armed CNA patrol crossed the frontier. C Tp dealt with the situation, forcing the Chinese soldiers back from whence they came. A week later the CNA repeated the incursion, with the same result. A CNA sergeant was arrested after drawing his side arm to threaten one of 44's sentries. A CNA officer was detected smuggling flour across the border. The incident escalated when the officer threatened 44's patrol with a primed grenade. After being disarmed he was duly arrested.

Shortly after this spate of incidents the GOC paid a visit to B Tp to assess this the latest outbreak of unrest initiated by the CNA. Again General Festing's diplomacy resulted in tensions being lowered. Almost as a sign of goodwill a column of 170 CNA troops with a horse train of 250 animals carrying sheaves of straw were allowed to cross the border into the Colony.

While the Commando was at Fan Ling the unit went through its greatest change in respect of movement of personnel. New drafts totalling 210 officers and men arrived in Hong Kong on board HM ships *Rajah*, *Venerable* and *Suffolk*. This influx of national servicemen replaced the hostilities only marines released for discharge. Coinciding with these exchanges further internal reorganisation resulted in the unit losing one rifle troop, the majority of X Tp being absorbed into the Heavy Weapons Troop (OC Capt H.Phillips). The Commando's rifle troops had, over a period of time, been reduced from the initial five to three. Amid these upheavals 44 paraded for an inspection by Brig B.W.Leicester DSO, RM (Officer Commanding, Commando Group).

June to September:

The Commando were relieved on the border by the newly arrived 45(RM)Commando with 44 subsequently transferring to Whitfield Barracks on Hong Kong island. The move was completed by 5th June. 'Royal' immediately started square bashing, brushing up the close order drill in readiness for a series of parades and other ceremonial duties. A detachment of 102 marines (Maj.J.A.Gilks) from the unit participated in the King's Birthday Parade at Happy Valley Racecourse on 13th June.

44's marines also provided Guards of Honour for the C-in-C (SEAC), General Sir Montague Stopford CB, DSO, MC at Kai Tak airfield on 15th July and Generals Lo Cho Ying (Governor of Canton) and Chang Fa Kwei (CNA) at Queens Pier, Hong Kong for the Generals' arrival and departure, 22nd and 24th August. His Excellency The Governor of Hong Kong (Sir Henry Seymore) conveyed a personal message of congratulations to the unit.

On 30th August the CO, Lt Col Price, commanded the Brigade contingent which marched in the 1946 Victory Parade. In recognition of the services rendered to the citizens of Hong Kong following the reoccupation of the colony, the Commando's RSM (WO1 J Spencer) was awarded the British Empire Medal (Military).

Aside from ceremonial duties 44's marines were used to guard Japanese POWs housed in Stanley Jail and assist members of the War Graves Commission in laying to rest the bodies of 410 Allied servicemen in Stanley Cemetery. The unit also aided the civil authorities in clearance work immediately following a particularly savage typhoon which wreaked havoc on the island on 18th July. The marines' barracks escaped unscathed with the exception of a few broken window panes.

The next day General Stopford paid an unofficial visit to the Commando, commending the marines on the effort put into the salvage operations carried out by the unit.

The training programme included 'Squeeze 1,' an assault landing exercise involving both 42 and 44(RM)Commandos. All troops carried out night exercises and A Tp added 'Seamanship' to their repertoire.

All troops plus the attached 3 Tp, 1/5 Commando also deployed to Stonecutters Island to use the weapon ranges. The unit also provided training facilities for HMS *Belfast's* Royal Marine detachment. The cruiser's marines spent 12 days with 44 before returning to the distinguished ship.

A sailing race, using 14 foot dinghies, between 42 and 44 resulted in the unit's yachtsmen coming a creditable second. Water sports became less popular following a shark attack on a swimmer in Stanley Bay. The incident involved a sergeant from the Signals troop who lost both legs. The unfortunate bather was admitted to Queen Mary's Hospital in a critical condition. Thanks to excellent medical attention, the man recovered and was discharged to the UK one month after the attack took place.

Lt Col Price relinquished command of the unit, being relieved by Lt Col P.R.Matters, RM on 19th September. On the last day of September the Brigade Commander, Brigadier H.D.Fellowes DSO, paid 44 a farewell visit before he too returned to the UK.

October to December:

The Commando relieved 45 in the New Territories on 1st/2nd October and carried on where they left off three months earlier, i.e, anti-smuggling patrols; raids on opium dens; frontier patrolling; anti-wood cutting patrols (the colony was still drastically short of timber); medical support included marines assisting local medical staff carrying out a vaccination programme in remote areas of the Colony.

20th November saw C Tp renewing old acquaintances with SS *Rajula*, the vessel responsible for creating 'Hortons Pirates.' The marines boarded the *Rajula* to restore order and to carry out the unenviable task of providing a guard on a group of CNA deserters. The Chinese soldiers had been guilty of causing a riot whilst on board the ship bound for Shanghai. C Tp returned to the unit on 11th December.

Brigadier P.H.G.Wills OBE, RM had superseded Brigadier Fellowes as Brigade Commander and wasted no time in visiting 44's locations in the New Territories shortly after his arrival in the colony. With the impending disbandment of 1/5 Army Commando in early 1947 the Brigadier would command an all Royal Marine Commando Brigade.

The new drafts of marines to the unit increased 44's compliment to such an extent that one of the extinct rifle troops was resurrected as Y Tp. The earlier tensions on the border had subsided considerably and the year drew to a close quietly.

Reorganisation 1947

In 1944 the Ministry of Labour and National Service was not the only department looking towards post-war reconstruction. An inter-service committee chaired by Air Marshal Sir Norman Bottomley (Deputy Chief of the Air Staff), concluded that the Royal Marines should resume the responsibility for all future amphibious operations: the Corps' traditional role! The committee's recommendations were ratified by Winston Churchill in August of that year but the die had been cast to bring about the demise of 44 (RM) Commando.

After the cessation of hostilities in August 1945 the Combined Chiefs of Staff assembled on 27th September to consider the future of the wartime Commando Forces. The conclusions reached by the most senior members of the three armed services were manifest; all existing Army Commando units would be disbanded. One Royal Marine Commando Brigade would be charged with providing an amphibious strike force for peacetime service. The basis of the Chiefs' decision focused on the outstanding factor that Army Commandos had been found from volunteers drawn from many units within the British Army. It was never intended to establish individual Commando units as permanent line regiments, all personnel being seconded from within the army after volunteering for 'duties of a hazardous nature.' The Green Beret identified a man as being a commando soldier, but unlike Royal Marines, who all shared the same cap badge, each individual commando soldier wore the badge of his parent regiment or corps.

Nevertheless, almost to a man, the soldiers considered the Commandos to be their regiment. When the Army Commandos were disbanded, all officers, NCOs and men were returned to their original units, many with a great feeling of sadness.

Major General R.E.Laycock DSO (Chief of Combined Operations) fought a futile battle to retain Commando forces within the Army structure. On 24th September 1945 he addressed the Army Commandos of 1 Commando Brigade to tell them of the decision to disband the wartime Commando Brigades. In an impassioned speech General Laycock told the assembled soldiers:

> Today there is no battle in store for you, nor have you lately fought one, yet nevertheless I am today more moved in speaking to you than ever before, for my emotions are not now those which I felt when I spoke to you in the past - the inspiration of battle and the exhilaration of coming danger - but they are deeper and more poignant emotions and they are these.

> First, the emotions of unbounded gratitude which I feel for every one of you who helped to make the Green Beret of the Commandos a symbol of bravery and honour whenever it has been worn. Secondly I am very conscious of the great privilege which I myself feel in having been associated with you and lastly, and most poignant of all, the emotions of sadness of farewell. For I have come here today to tell you, on the instructions of the Prime Minister and of the Chiefs of Staff, the Commando Group, most probably the finest fighting formation in the world, is now to be disbanded and that the Green Beret is a thing of war and not of peace.

> When you have gone it will be worn no more; for I do not propose that others shall be allowed to wear that distinctive headress which by rights is yours and yours alone.

> It shall be kept in trust as the emblem of your corps d'elite until the day, if it ever comes, when the Commando Group shall be reformed to meet the needs of the Nation at war... the work which you have done in developing a special technique has not been done in vain. That technique will be kept alive in the experimental and training establishments of the Combined Operations Command by personnel of the Royal Marines set apart for that duty: but they will not wear the Green Beret because that part of your uniform, as I have already told you, is to be kept in trust for the Commando Group of the future for, if

ever we go to war again, which God forbid, you can bet your
bottom dollar that Commando Group will be reformed...

Gentlemen, the word Commando is to me at once the finest and
most glorious in the English language. It is a word which will
never die in the annals of war.

In respect of the Green Beret, General Laycock's pledge was
overruled by higher authority. Lord Louis Mountbatten's intrinsic
attachment to Commando forces, linked together with his Royal Naval
background, of which the Royal Marines are part, undoubtedly ensured
that the post-war commandos would continue to wear the famed
headress. Lord Louis was loyally supported by Major General
Wildman-Lushington who had been so active behind the scenes to
ensure that his Corps of Royal Marines would reclaim its traditional
mantle, evoking to the full the marines motto 'Per Mare, Per Terram' -
by Sea, by Land.

With the exception of 1/5 Army and 42, 44 and 45 Royal Marine, all
other Commando units, both Army and Royal Marine had been
disbanded during the early months of 1946. With no prospect of 3
Commando Brigade being brought back to the United Kingdom in the
immediate future, a decision was taken that the Brigade would carry
the banner of Commando forces into the future. 1/5 Commando
gradually reduced in size as its personnel were released for discharge,
45 taking over the Army Commando's responsibilities. 1/5 were finally
disbanded on 31st December 1946.

Initially it had been assumed that the Brigade would retain four
Commandos in keeping with wartime establishments. The
Commandant General Royal Marines (General Sir Thomas Hunton)
proposed that new unit identification numbers would be representative
of Royal Marine Commando units of all the four wartime Commando
Brigades thus:

    1 Commando Brigade: 45 (RM) Commando

    2 Commando Brigade: 40 (RM) Commando

    3 Commando Brigade: 42 (RM) Commando

    4 Commando Brigade: 41 (RM) Commando

However the establishment laid down for the peacetime 3
Commando Brigade was for three Commando units and the
Commandant General's original proposals were amended. The revised
unit numbers being representative of one Royal Marine Commando

engaged in each of the three main theatres of war.

40 (RM) Commando: The Mediterranean.

42 (RM) Commando: The Far East.

45 (RM) Commando: Europe.

It is not recorded why 44 was chosen to be renumbered in preference to 42 but the fate of the unit was sealed on 20th February when it was resolved that 44 would be re-christened to become 40(RM) Commando.

40 Commando had been raised in Deal on 14th February 1942. Initially the unit was known as the Royal Marine 'A' Commando (until 29th October, 1942). The Commando first saw action during the ill-fated amphibious raid on Dieppe in August 1942 where the unit sustained heavy casualties. After the marines had been re-equipped 40 was transferred to 2 Special Service Brigade, serving alongside Nos 2 and 9 Army plus 43 (RM) Commandos in Italy and along the Adriatic coast.

Renumbering parade: 44 becomes 40 (RM) Commando. The CO, Lt Col R D Houghton MC, RM addresses the parade. Col Houghton was awarded the Military Cross for his services with 40 Commando at Dieppe, where he was captured and made a POW. The adjutant, Capt Aldridge, faces the Colonel.

On 15th March 1947, shortly before the Brigade, under the command of Brig D.W.Leicester DSO, RM redeployed to Malta, 44 (RM) Commando ceased to exist. At a simple ceremony in Hong Kong, the unit's flag was lowered for the last time and replaced by the pennant of the resurrected 40(RM)Commando (Lt Col R.D.Houghton MC RM). The men of 44 had been transferred into the first of the nine Royal Marine Commandos raised during World War II.

44 had proudly upheld the traditions of the Royal Marines. From the time that the Commando had been raised from the 3rd Battalion, Royal Marines, the men had carried out their duties in a manner befitting members of their Corps.

During the Commando course at Achnacarry the rigorous and demanding training weeded out those men considered unsuitable to serve as Commando soldiers and also claimed the lives of three marines. On board the '*Reina Del*' the Commando had been party to one of the very first air attacks in which the Luftwaffe used the lethal Glider Bomb.

After acclimatising to the tropical temperatures and humid conditions the Commando had been the first unit of the Brigade to land on the Arakan coast. At Alethangyaw 44's marines gained first hand experience in opposing a barbarous, devious and dedicated enemy. From the early days, the unit rapidly adapted to the dank jungle conditions, using the dense jungle vegetation to spring surprise attacks on an unsuspecting enemy. The men became oblivious to the bloated leeches, some six or eight inches long which clung to the skin, the jungle sores, fever and the debilitating ravages of malaria.

The interminable railway journeys through India, with the ever frequent halts to transfer stores and equipment between trains running on lines of different gauges, tried the patience and humour of the most dedicated.

44's marines were forced to wade waist high through the thickest and deepest mud to effect a landing at Myebon. At Kangaw the Commando sustained as many casualties as any other unit, winning the admiration of the Brigade in respect of their stubborn defence of 'Pinner' early in the campaign. In Hong Kong 44 prosecuted their sometimes difficult and sensitive duties with tact, understanding and on some occasions, studied resolution.

Her Majesty the Queen approved 38 battle honours to the Commando Association and these can be seen on the Association's 'battle honours' standard laid up in St George's Chapel, Westminster Abbey (situated by the Great West Door). In the Nave immediately adjacent to the chapel is a memorial to the Mountbattens, the stone lying within a few yards of the Commando's battle standard. Four of the honours commemorate the Brigade's engagements: Alethangyaw, Myebon, Kangaw and Burma 1943-45.

To paraphrase 'Kilroy,' 44 (Royal Marine) Commando was there!

Another memorial to World War II Commando Forces can be found in the abbey. A bronze statue of a Commando stands in the West Cloister between similar figures depicting a Submariner and an Airborne Soldier. The inscription beneath the commando reads, 'They performed whatsoever the King commanded.'

Above the entrance to the West Cloister is a large imposing memorial to General George Wade. Military roads constructed by Wade during the early years of the eighteenth century, traversed the Highlands in the area around Achnacarry. No doubt many would-be Commandos marched along these same roads whilst attending the training course at the depot.

Maj Gen Horton (extreme right) celebrates with his officers and marines at a reunion in London during the 1970s.

The Commando produced two future major generals, Royal Marines: Frank Cyril Horton CB, OBE was born in 1907 and was commissioned into the Corps in 1925. His first 15 years of service were spent at sea in ships of the Royal Navy. Joining HMS *Cumberland* in 1928 as a young officer, he served first on the China Station before transferring to the Mediterranean Fleet (HMS *Royal Oak*). In 1936 Cyril Horton joined HMS *Ajax* on the sunny Americas/West Indies Station. After the outbreak of war he was recalled to the UK and attended the Staff College, Camberley before being promoted lieutenant colonel after which he served on the staff of the Chief of Combined Operations. Lt Col Horton was a highly respected and admired commanding officer of 44 during 1943/44. When Frank Horton left the Commando at Teknaf in November 1944 he returned home to take up a position on the directing staff at Camberley. After the war ended the Colonel was appointed to a number of positions: The Plans Division at the Admiralty; Directing Staff, Joint Services Staff College; Commandant, Royal Marines School of Amphibious Warfare; Staff of the Imperial Defence College; Colonel (GS), Staff of Commandant General, RM; Chief of Staff to Commandant General, Royal Marines. Major General Horton received his final promotion in 1955 and he retired from the Corps in 1958.

John Ivor Headon Owen OBE was born in 1922 and joined the Royal Marines as a marine recruit in 1942. The Corps, quick to spot talent, commissioned 2nd Lieutenant Owen the same year, posting the young officer to 3rd Battalion, Royal Marines. John Owen served throughout the war years with 44, gaining promotion to captain in June 1945. He was 'demobbed' in 1946 and immediately joined the Metropolitan Police in the rank of constable. Colonel Drysdale happened upon his protégé pounding the beat and later, with Colonel Horton, persuaded the young policeman that his future lay with the Corps. To re-enlist ex-Captain Owen dropped a rank, rejoining as a lieutenant in 1947. The following seven years were spent on regimental service before Captain Owen was seconded to the Staff College, Camberley. From 1959-62 John Owen held the appointment of Brigade Major, 3 Commando Brigade after which came a two year spell in the Department of Naval Plans at the Admiralty. Commando service was resumed with 42 (1964-66) to be followed by a period as an instructor at the Joint Services Staff College and promotion to lieutenant colonel. As the commanding officer of 45 (1967-68) Lt Col Owen was mentioned in despatches during the Commando's tour of duty in Aden. 45 were the last British servicemen to leave the protectorate, the CO was almost the last man to depart. Following in the steps of of his mentor, Colonel Owen later served as Colonel (GS) on the Staff of the Commandant General, Royal Marines. The real life rags to riches story was completed in 1972 when John Owen was appointed Major General, Commando Forces, Royal Marines. The young lieutenant had joined the Brigade (as a founder member) in 1943; 30 years later General Owen was to command Britain's Amphibious Strike Force. Cyril Horton and Douglas Drysdale had been right!

Lt Col D.B.Drysdale DSO, RM, a one time commanding officer of 44 went on to greater glory commanding 41 (Independent) Commando RM in Korea. This small unit of approximately 300 men left Britain in September 1950 and after mounting several successful raids against North Korean lines of communication running along the north-eastern coast, joined the US 1st Marine Division. The Commandos fought an epic rearguard action in minus temperatures during the Division's fighting retreat south, an action recognised by the then US President who awarded a Presidential Unit Citation to the 1st Marine Division, USMC. Initially 41 were excluded from the citation as the Royal Marines were a 'foreign unit.' However an executive order was made on 10th January, 1957 abolishing the restriction relating to foreign units and Douglas Drysdale's 41 was added to the citation. A unique distinction and honour.

9
Sport

Sport in general and football in particular was the ultimate morale booster. At troop, unit and brigade levels, 44's footballers always played the game with enthusiasm and skill. The unit football team first came to prominence shortly after the Commando was established at Ashurst. The representative side beat Southampton Town 2-0. Following 44's return from Achnacarry, the unit's super fit footballers played Folkestone Town on two occasions. After losing the first game, the marines took their revenge, winning the return fixture 5-1.

After reaching India and adjusting to camp life at Kedgaon, time was found to mark out a football pitch. As soon as the white lines were dry and the goal posts set up, the inter-troop (two teams per troop) football league was established. The Commando eleven represented the unit against the marines attached to the Mobile Naval Base Defence Organisation (MNBDO) at Galunshi, drawing the match 0-0. They also played 11 RM before that battalion returned home, winning 4-2.

Operation Screwdriver plus long periods of jungle patrolling at Silkuri took their toll when the representative team resumed playing soccer. In June 1944 44 lost two consecutive matches against the airmen of 168 Wing RAF. The marines sought revenge. It came on the waterlogged pitch at Silchar, 44 winning by the only goal of the match. No doubt the amphibious background of the Commando team helped them cope with the wet conditions. The Commando team travelled to Kumbhirgram for the return fixture winning the game 2-1. Not happy to see 'Royal' beating their colleagues, 189 Wing, RAF fielded a side against 44. The marines were the victors (5-4) after a hard fought game.

With 44's marines having the edge over the RAF at football, the airmen tried rugby. A combined 168/189 Wing RAF team played the Commando, again on a flooded pitch and honours were shared, the result 0-0.

Whilst assigned to locations in and around Silchar, 44 fielded a side against the local tea planters. Although the marines won the match 6-0, the game was a brutal affair, with bruised, grazed and swollen legs confirming that the planters took no prisoners where football was concerned.

In an inter-troop game, the CO watched D and S Tps beat A and B Tps 7-3; while a combined officers/SNCO's eleven held the might of Brigade HQ to a 1-1 draw.

July's hot wet monsoon weather had reduced the number of football matches played to a minimum: The Commando team thrashed 189 Wing RAF 9-0. S Tp played 1 Commando's 1 Tp, which resulted in a 1-1 draw and in another inter-unit fixture 44's officers lost to 5's officers 5-0.

By August 1944, 5 and 44 Commandos had moved down to Bangalore where the majority of men from both units were granted 14 days leave. The marines that remained in camp turned out a scratch side to play their counterparts in 5. The soldiers left some of their best footballers in camp and 44 were humiliated, losing 5-0. Before leaving for Trincomalee, 44, at full strength, played RAF Bangalore; the match drawn 2-2.

In 'Trinco' Football dominated the sporting scene. After taking six months to arrange, the match that everyone had eagerly anticipated was played; 44 v 5. With both Commandos turning out a full strength side, the game was well supported by marines and soldiers from each unit. As expected the game was hard fought: the marines finally winning the match 3-1.

44's football team, Ceylon, Sept 1944. Back row (l-r): Cpl. Mick Kelly (Capt); Sgt Ted Mylett; Sgt Albert Lamb; Sgt Jack Johnson; Cpl Taff Headon. Front row (l-r): Mne Joe Cooper; Cpl Johnny McLeish; Cpl Tommy Sims; Mne Bill Deakin; Sgt Bill Amor; Mne Jock Goulden.

During their stay in Ceylon 44 also played 42 Commando, winning 6-2. Three games were played against RM Engineers, where the honours were shared, both teams winning one match with one game drawn. A charity match v RM Engineers (Prisoner of War Relief Fund), 44 winning the game 1-0. HMS *Renown*, whose ship's team inflicted a rare defeat on 44's marines winning in some style, 2-0. 'Royal' gained some revenge against the Royal Navy by beating HMS *Adamant* 3-0. Once again the match was played on a flooded pitch. In the only game of hockey played, 44's officers and SNCOs lost 4-0 to their counterparts in 42.

A person unknown deemed that the cricket season had arrived, necessitating a trial match to be played; the unit's cricketers turned out in force.

At Teknaf the Commando played two important football matches in the period leading up to Christmas 1944. The game against 1 Commando was a very hard and thrilling contest, the final result being a 2-2 draw. The Commando team then went on to easily beat their fellow marines of 42 by 4 goals to 2.

When the unit returned to Akyab following the Brigade's involvement at Kangaw and subsequent raiding operations along the Arakan coast, many of 44's marines picked up the netball bug once more. However, the game had, by now, secured the more macho name of basketball. In the final of the unit knockout competition, the heavy weapons men of S Tp were victorious over B Tp.

All elements of the Brigade entered teams in the swimming gala also held in Akyab. On the day 44 were pipped at the post by their old sporting adversaries 5 Commando: Brigade HQ took third place, followed by 42 and 1. Maj Gen G.E.Wildman-Lushington CBE (a Royal Marine and Assistant Chief of Staff, Supreme Commander, SEAC) who was visiting the Brigade at the time watched as 44 and 5 competed with their customary good humour and honest rivalry.

Following the move back to India in April 1945, the Commando football team had the satisfaction of beating 42 (1-0), shortly before the Brigade relocated to Ahmadnager. Despite the intense heat and humidity experienced at Ahmadnagar, 5 and 44 continued their battle on the football pitch. In another keenly fought and exciting game the marines maintained their unbeaten record against the soldiers, winning the game 2-1. 'Royal' had an easier game against a Royal Armoured Corp side, winning that game quite comfortably 12-0.

When the unit returned to Ahmadnagar from the jungle warfare training course at Londa, football was dominated by the inter-troop, Horton Cup competition: a trophy donated by Lt Col F.C.Horton. Teams representing all 44's Troops, plus teams of both officers and SNCOs participated in the keenly contested knockout competition. The final between S and C Tps was played on 14th June, the heavy weapons Troop defeating C Troop 2-0. The cup was presented to the winning captain by the CO, Lt Col Drysdale.

X Tp, Horton Cup Winners, Hong Kong

5 Commando, never ones to take defeat lightly, challenged 44 to yet another football match (the fourth). After the usual hard tussle, the marines came out on top, winning 4-2.

By far the most exciting match played at Ahmadnagar was between the two Royal Marines Commandos. 42 took an early 3-1 lead, 44 pulled the score back to 3-3 and an honourable draw looked a certain result. However 44 managed to score a last minute winning goal. 42(RM) Commando was not amused!

At Karakvasla where the Brigade were busy training for the impending landings in Malaya, sport took a back seat. However the Brigade's football team played two representative matches with the team being built around seven players from 44. The Brigade side putting up two very credible performances; v Poona Select: winning 2-0 and v 29 Brigade, drawing 3-3.

During the early months in Hong Kong the all-conquering Commando football team remained unbeaten. The team played HMS *Venerable* winning 11-0; Eastern Athletic Association winning 7-1 and HMS *Nabcatcher* winning 3-2.

In two matches against HMS *Anson*, the first match was drawn 3-3, the marines winning the second game 7-0.

Despite changes to the Commando brought about by men returning to the UK for demobilisation the unit's football team still flourished.

After beating HMS *Montclare* 1-0, the Commando team played the Police side from the neighbouring Portuguese free port of Macao. The fixture generated great interest in the Colony and a match commentary was broadcast 'live' by the local radio station. In a high scoring game 44 came out the winners 8-3.

The Commando team went on to play a much stronger Chinese XI in Hong Kong, the two sides drawing the game 1-1.

In addition to the representative matches, the unit footballers once again competed for the Horton Cup. In a thrilling final X and S Tps drew 1-1 after extra time. In the replay X Tp were victorious, winning 2-0. The cup was presented by the commanding officer.

The unit's soccer stars were selected to play in various representative sides. Lt R.R.Jack and Cpl Headon played in the Combined Services side v Combined Chinese XI (2-4). Troop Sergeant Majors Smith and Johnson together with Sgt Wilkes played for the 'Mainland' side versus Hong Kong Island, (4-0).

By the middle of 1946 the unit football team began to lose matches. 44's post war teams were never able to emulate the wartime successes of the Commando's footballers.

44's representative soccer team (1943-45) was unsurpassed in 3 Commando Brigade. It took a very good side to beat it: not many did!

Postscript

3 (Wartime) Commando Brigade stood drawn up in Commando formations on the former parade ground of the now defunct Eastney Royal Marine Barracks. The renovated brickwork of the old barrack blocks facing the sea (recently converted into luxury apartments) together with the imposing facade of the old officers' mess, in which the Royal Marines Museum has been accommodated, provided a worthy backdrop for the day's events. Approximately 230 ex-Commandos had marched on in brilliant hot sunshine led by the Band of HM Royal Marines (Portsmouth) watched by 30 who through age or illness could not participate. Every man was dressed in the rig of the day: Green Beret, Corps/Regimental cap badge and tie, blue blazer with medals, grey trousers and needless to say; glistening shoes.

The guest list was impressive: Commandant General Royal Marines: Lt Gen Sir Robert Ross KCB, OBE; The President, Commando Association, Lt Col A.R.Evill (South Wales Borderers); Director, Royal Marines Museum, Col K.N.Wilkins OBE; Lord Mayor of Portsmouth, Cllr Malcolm Chewter; Leader, Hampshire County Council, Cllr Mike Hancock CBE; Ex-Bishop of Norwich, Rt Rev M.A.P.Wood DSC, MA, RNR; Lt Col R.Wright OBE MC (19th King George V's Own Lancers).

The President of the Commando Association (Lt Col Evill) accompanied by Maj Gen J.I.H.Owen OBE (ex 44 Commando), the Commandant General, Brig K.R.S.Trevor CBE, DSO (ex 1 Commando) and the parade commander Capt H.J.Phillips OBE, QPM reviewed the parade, pausing at regular intervals to chat to old comrades.

After the President had returned to the saluting dais, seven Royal Marine Buglers plus the bass drummer marched from the Band's ranks, stacking their drums to create the traditional battlefield altar.

The Service of Remembrance and Thanksgiving was conducted by the Rt Rev Wood (ex-44 Commando). Proudly wearing his Green Beret, Maurice Wood led the assembled veterans plus some 450 relatives and friends in prayer. Sombre though the service was, the Bishop added a degree of humour to the proceedings, especially reminding 44 of the many occasions that he had preached to them in the Far East.

As the concluding notes of the Last Post faded, signalling the start of the Solemn Silence, the gathering became quiet, the hush casting a complete calm over the parade. Not one cough or spoken word disturbed the moment as those congregated together remembered the 143 soldiers and marines who gave up their lives during the Brigade's battles against the Japanese enemy. When the Royal Marine Buglers sounded the Naval Reveille, 'Charlie, Charlie, lash up and stow,' a huge sigh was released and many a tear was wiped from the eye.

The Brigade had been standing for an hour before the order was given to move off in column of threes to march past the saluting base. The average age of the old soldiers and marines on parade was well over seventy years and to their eternal credit each man bore the heat of the day without complaint. Two veterans were overcome by the hot weather and assisted from the ranks during the service. One would not be denied his place in the ranks, returning to his Commando to take part in the march past. The other man who had, incidentally, undergone triple by-pass heart surgery took note of the old adage 'Discretion is the better part of valour' and remained in the beer tent.

With Brigade Headquarters in the van, the Commandos marched past the reviewing officer (Lt Col Evill), with a measured tread and bags of swank. Each unit was gently escorted along the route of march by a serving Army or Royal Marine Drill Instructor; the veterans being warmly applauded by the many onlookers as they passed by.

44 was the final unit in the column and provided the largest contingent, some 80 officers, NCOs and marines. As 44's marines neared the public enclosure the band struck up the Commando March 'Sarie Marais.' To the strains of 'Give me my gun and my fighting knife' the 'First Drill', gave the command '44 Commando - left wheel.' The music changed to the Regimental March, 'A Life on the Ocean Wave' as 44 marched past the dais. Eighty Royal Marines re-kindled the snap, bearing and precision of yesteryear for the benefit of the Commando Association's President, the assembled guests and the multitude of relatives and friends who had travelled to Southsea from all over the British Isles and several countries beyond to be part of a very special and moving occasion.

Within the Corps there is a maxim which states that there is no such thing as an 'Ex' Royal Marine: 'once a Royal Marine always a Royal Marine.' On 13th August 1995, 44 (Royal Marine) Commando proved the point!

ROLL OF HONOUR
Killed in Action Alethangyaw, March 1944
Rev H.C.W.Manger RNVR

Lt J.A.McKinnon

Sgt Hodnett

Sgt R.D.Grant

Cpl J.R.Bedford

L/Cpl G.Gigg

Killed in Action Kangaw, January 1945
Capt A.Martin

Cpl A.V.Bowen

Cpl R.F.Fleming

Cpl G.T.Hesp

Cpl P.Kirby

Cpl A.A.Marshall

Cpl A.E.Williams

L/Cpl F.Foot

L/Cpl A.Heath

L/Cpl J.Mustow

L/Cpl L.W.Payne

L/Cpl L.Richardson

Mne J.M.Ashworth

Mne G.E.Beach

Mne E.C.Bolam

Mne V.Edwards

Mne F.G.Lewis

Mne D.McDonald

Mne J.Morrison

Mne C.E.Palmer

Mne J.Pinkney

Mne D.Scott

Mne A.J.Sheather

Mne D.Shore

Mne J.N.Stockwell

Mne J.W.Ternent

Mne S.K.Walters

Died on Active Service
Mne S.Daly

Mne C.W.Haw

Mne D.Nelson

Mne J.O'Reilly

Mne E.Polkinhorne

Mne W.J.Watkins

Rolls of Officers

June 1944
Commanding Officer: Lt Col F.C.Horton
2 I/C: vacant
Adjutant: Capt K.P.Parish
Captains
O.St John Hamlin
A.V.Macan
A.Martin
R.C.Steele
E.M.Sturges
C.A.Watkins
Lieutenants
R.G.Acton
A.E.Barrett
G.P.A.Bleasdell
C.N.C.Carryer
S.Henshall
P.T.A.Musters
J.I.H.Owen
A.K.Powrie
P.H.Rider
P.Shefford
G.D.Stewart
A.R.White
S.G.Wintgens

December 1944
Commanding Officer: Lt Col G.H.Stockley
2 I/C: Major H.G.S.Saunders
Adjutant: Capt K.P.Parish
Captains
O.St John Hamlin
S.C.Hellis
A.V.Macan
A.Martin
E.M.Sturges
C.A.Watkins
Lieutenants
R.G.Acton
A.E.Barrett

G.P.A.Bleasdell
W.W.H.Brydon
C.N.C.Carryer
S.Henshall
D.H.Lewis
P.T.A.Musters
J.I.H.Owen
A.K.Powrie
P.H.Rider
P.Shefford
A.R.White

June 1945
Commanding Officer: Lt Col D.B.Drysdale MBE
2 I/C: Major H.R.Burton
Adjutant: Capt C.A.Watkins
Captains
R.G.Acton
D.F.Furlong
J.A.Gilks
J.E.C.Howarth
A.V.Macan
K.P.Parish
Lieutenants
F.E.Bates
D.E.Clilverd
S.L.Fouché (SAUDF)
D.N.Fuoss
J.G.Gray
J.H.Holyoake
H.G.Hough
R.R.Jack
J.K.Lee
D.H.Lewis
J.I.H.Owen
E.A.R.Syms
J.A.Smith
P.E.Towhill
D.C.Tremlett

December 1945
Commanding Officer: Lt Col N.P.Wood
2 I/C: Major C.L.Price
Adjutant: Capt C.A.Watkins
Major: J.A.Gilks
Captains
R.G.Acton
D.F.Furlong
A.V.Macan
J.I.H.Owen
J.A.Smith
Lieutenants
J.B.Blacklaws
G.P.A.Bleasdell
D.E.Clilverd
A.E.Elliott
H.G.Hough
R.R.Jack
D.H.Lewis
H.H.Orpen
H.J.Phillips
E.A.R.Syms
G.B.Ticehurst
D.C.Tremlett
J.F.White

Officers' movements 1944/45

DRAFTED IN	DRAFTED OUT
Ashurst	
Capt P.B.S.Baxter	
Capt F.A.Farquharson Roberts	
Capt E.Langley	
Lt F.T.Cousins	
Lt G.A.Kaye	
Achnacarry	**Achnacarry**
Lt P.Dexter	Capt F.A.Farquharson Roberts
	Capt G.P.E.Sealey
	Lt K.A.Abbs
	Lt A.H.Archer
	Lt T.L.Hughes
	Lt W.J.Standing

Folkestone
Lt G.P.A.Bleasdell
Lt D.H.Lewis
Lt A.K.Powrie
2/Lt J.A.Mackinnon
2/Lt T.Shefford
2/Lt G.B.Stewart
Kedgaon
Lt R.G.Acton
Lt W.W.H.Brydon

Silchar
Capt K.Martin
Capt N.J.Winter
Silkuri
Capt T.C.Coole

Bangalore
Capt H.G.S.Saunders
Trincomalee
Maj G.E.Stockley
Capt S.C.Hellis
Lt A.P.O'Brien

Trincomalee
Maj J.L.A.Macafee
Lt G.D.Stewart

Teknaf
Lt Col F.C.Horton
Capt R.G.Steele
Lt S.G.Wintgens
Myebon
Maj H.G.S.Saunders

Myebon
Maj H.F.C.Kimpton
Nasik
Four Subalterns
Poona
Lt Col D.B.Drysdale
Plus three officers

Poona
Lt Col G.E.Stockley
Capt E.M.Sturges
Lt S.Henshall
Lt A.P.O'Brien
Lt A.K.Powrie
Lt A.R.White

Madras Three subalterns
Ahmadnagar

Lt S.L.Fouché (SAUDF)
Lt J.H.Holyoake
Lt J.A.Smith

Ahmadnagar
Maj H.R.Burton
Capt S.C.Hellis
Lt W.R.Bayliss
2/Lt K.W.J.Browning
2/Lt A.W.Warltair

Kharakvasla
Maj P.Wood
Lt J.B.Blacklaws
Lt M.T.Deenham
Lt A.L.Elliott
Lt E.L.Marsh
Lt I.N.McColm
Lt H.J.Phillips
Lt D.H.Ranger MBE (SAUDF)
Lt G.B.Ticehurst
Lt F.Tunstall

Kowloon
Maj C.L.Price
Lt G.P.A.Bleasdell (rejoined)
Lt D.H.Lewis (rejoined)
Lt J.F.White

Kharakvasla
Capt K.P.Parish
Capt O.St John Hamlin
Lt P.E.Bates
Lt D.H.Fuoss
Lt D.H.Lewis

Londa
Lt P.T.A.Masters
Lt R.L.Worsfold

Kowloon
Lt Col D.B.Drysdale
Capt J.E.Howarth
Lt S.L.Fouché (SAUDF)
Lt J.K.Lee

Senior officers visits/inspections

Name/rank/appointment	Date
FM Lord Alanbrook, CIGS	16/11/45
Lt Gen F.A.Browning DSO, Chief of Staff, Supreme Comdr SEAC	19/12/44
Maj Gen A.R.Chater CB, DSO, RM, Director, Combined Ops, Far East	4/12/44
Lt Gen Sir A.F.P.Christison KBE, CB, MC, GOC, XV Indian Corps	2/11/44
	26/12/44
	27/2/45
	26/7/45
Col R.F.Cornwall MBE, RM, Staff, SEAC Headquarters	15/3/44
Maj Gen F.W.Festing DSO, GOC 29th Infantry Div	26/12/44

Maj Gen F.W.Festing CB, CBE, DSO, GOC Land Forces
Hong Kong   29/8/45
                                                       25/9/45
                                                        6/11/45
                                                       29/11/45
                                                       25/12/45
                                                       13/2/46
                                                       15/4/46
                                                       20/5/46

Maj Gen E.N.Goddard CBE, MVO, MC, GOC Local Area
'Ahmadnagar'   9/6/45

Rear Adml C.J.Harcourt CB, CBE, RN, C-in-C
Hong Kong   25/9/45

Brig J.E.Hirst DSO, GOC 74 Brigade, 25 Ind Div   7/11/44

Maj Gen Kwok, Chinese Nationalist Army   15/4/46

Maj Gen R.E.Laycock DSO, Chief of Combined Ops   4/12/44

BrigB.W.Leicester DSO, RM, OC Commando Group   24/4/46

Maj Gen G.E.Lomax CB, CBE, DSO, MC
GOC 26 Ind Div   23/12/44
                                                       30/4/45

Adml Lord Louis Mountbatten, Supreme Allied Comdr
SEAC   23/1/44
                                                       19/12/44
                                                        4/2/46

Col C.F.Phillips DSO, RM, Senior RM officer, British
Pacific Fleet   29/1/46

Maj Gen R.P.L.Renkin CBE, MC, GOC Local Area
'Silkuri'   2/5/44

Lt Gen O.L.Roberts CB, CBE, DSO, GOC 34 Ind Corps   19/4/45
                                                       20/5/45

Lt Gen M.G.N.Stopford CB, DSO, MC, GOC 33 Ind Corps 4/1/44

Gen Sir Montague Stopford, C-in-C SEAC   19/7/46

Maj Gen R.G.Sturges CB, DSO, RM, GOC Special Service
Group   16/9/43

Maj Gen G.E.Wildman-Lushington CBE, RM
Asst Chief of Staff, Supreme Comdr SEAC   28/2/45

Maj Gen G.E.Wildman-Lushington CBE, RM
GOC Commando Group   28/8/45

Maj Gen G.N.Wood OBE, MC, GOC 25th Ind Div   5/1/45

Bibliography

Books

The Commandos 1940-1946 Charles Messenger
The Green Beret Hilary St John Saunders
The Royal Marines Maj Gen J.L.Moulton
Commandos and Rangers of WW2 James Ladd
Castle Commando Donald Gilchrist
The Lee Enfield Rifle Major E.G.B.Reynolds
The Lee Enfield Story Ian Skennerton
Official History Indian Armed Forces in WW2, Arakan Ops 1942-1945
Bisheshwar Prasad
Official History WW2: The War Against Japan Vol IV. HMSO.
Defeat into Victory Field Marshal Lord 'Bill' Slim
Imperial Gazetteer: India 1908. Official
A History of Hong Kong Frank Welsh
An Illustrated History of Hong Kong Nigel Cameron

Journal

The Jungle Book: Magazine of 3 Cdo Brigade: Nos. 3, 5, 7, 8, 9

Others

Who's Who
Lloyd's List
*Report to Combined Chiefs of Staff Supreme Allied Commander South East
Asia Command*

Public Record Office

Reference	Short title
ADM202/95	44(RM) Commando War Diary
ADM202/96	44(RM) Commando War Diary
ADM202/97	44(RM) Commando War Diary
ADM199/1317	*Reina Del Pacifico*
ADM199/1318	Convoy KMF 26
ADM199/2146	Sinking of *Rohna*
DEFE2/50	Sinking of *Rohna*
DEFE2/554	Operation 'Screwdriver' (No.5 Cdo Ops)
DEFE2/569	Naval Report--LCP's
DEFE2/764	Com Ops Landing Ships
DEFE2/843	Commando Casualties
DEFE2/1041	RM Commandos, 3 (SS) Brigade Overseas
DEFE2/1105	Requirement for Commandos in S.E.Asia
DEFE2/1116	COPP Reports, History
DEFE2/1325	Disbandment of Cdo Group
DEFE2/1336	RM Cdos Post War Policy, Organisation, Training
DEFE2/1343	Commando Group Reorganisation: duties Far East
LAB32/12	'De-mob' formula
LAB32/14	ditto
LAB32/37	Section 'B' release
WO203/1	Assault Beaches: Op"Zipper"
WO203/23	Assault Landing: Akyab
WO203/67	War Diaries No. 5 Commando
WO203/1792	3 SS Bde. Report on Ops
WO203/1989	Arakan Operations
WO203/2940	3 SS Bde Movements
WO203/4279	Re-occupation, Hong Kong
WO203/4359	ditto (Correspondence)
WO203/4802	Employment Commando Brigade